# the meaning of Truth

## embrace your truth. create your life.

## Nicole J. Sachs, LCSW

*2nd Edition*

Safe Harbor Press
Re: The Meaning of Truth
110 Angler's Road, Suite 105
Lewes, DE 19958
www.meaningoftruthbook.com
ISBN: 1482387352
ISBN 13: 9781482387353


Printed in the United States of America

"During times of universal deceit,
telling the truth becomes a revolutionary act."
GEORGE ORWELL

*For My Mother,*
*Who first showed me how to notice the truth.*

*And for Tiffany,*
*Who, in light of this, introduced me to myself.*

# Forward to the Second Edition

When I first published this book, I was scared. I was mostly scared that you wouldn't hear me. That it was impossible for people to believe that an emotional exercise could literally cure a myriad of physical symptoms, disorders and chronic conditions. I felt compelled to write it, but I panicked the whole time that I wouldn't be heard. I apologized for interrupting your life to impose this life-saving insight. I begged you repeatedly to hear me out. I threw myself in front of your moving car and screamed, "But I can save your life if you just pull over and pay attention!"

In the years since I published the first edition of *The Meaning of Truth*, I have had the benefit of working with hundreds of patients and communicating with many more. I'm not scared anymore. I've seen far too many people crawl through my door on disability or suicidal as a result of their pain, and leave treatment as fully functional pain-free humans. I know that this will cure you, if you want to be cured.

I say this because I've learned another thing in my years of treating people in the grips of chronic conditions - people are compelled to hold onto their pain for reasons they often don't recognize. Perhaps their pain helps them to feel deserving of care and connection. Perhaps they are able to ask for help from others when they are hurting enough, and they fear that they will be all alone if this is removed. Maybe they long to trust authority, and putting their lives into the hands of doctors, surgeons and pharmaceuticals feels oddly safer than trying something that puts them behind the wheel. Maybe the way they've been handling things is simply the only way they've ever known.

Regardless of the reason, I understand. I have been you. I sat right there in that personal hell of hopelessness and despair, and I found a way out. I know that each of us holds the key to the jail in which we sit. I also know that it's really hard to envision that kind of personal power. I offer you the chance to do something different, and create a life free of chronic pain and conditions.

When I give lectures to groups of people aching with chronic pain, I like to look into the crowd and ask them the question, "How long would you like to suffer?" I do this not to disparage the seriousness of your situation, or mock you as if you are choosing it. I ask you this question to wake you up. To hand you back your choices. To let you know that although this might not work for everyone, I'm quite certain that it can work for *you*.

So, here's your opportunity to heal. I'm not begging you, I'm telling you straight up: If you want to be free of this misery, you can be. Open your mind, quiet your fear, remember that you don't know everything, and give yourself the chance to live. I am here to help you, and I know you can do it.

With love,

Nicole

# Table of Contents

# I am a therapist

I am more than that. I am a mother, a partner, a really good friend, a saver and a fixer. I am really needy sometimes. I am vulnerable and raw, then embarrassed that I let myself be seen. I am strong and stubborn more than necessary. I'm so in love with love, it has hurt me. I'm so in love with love, it has saved me. I try too hard. I am obsessed with my children's happiness. I am overwhelmed by the demands of motherhood. I am fueled by admiration. I am lifted by people brave enough to say they are not brave. At times I wish everyone would just leave me alone. I am full of gratitude. I am scared I will never be good enough. I am eternally hopeful.

I am a human being. So are you.

When you feel resistance, try to be curious enough to listen to me.

When you feel stuck and exhausted, know that I am here with you.

When you find it impossible to believe what I propose, read this whole book and then ask yourself again.

When you need inspiration, I will tell you my story another time. Or somebody else's who is generous enough to join us. I will remind you that I am human just like you, right by your side. I am no better because I am sitting on this side of the couch. Once you "get" what I'm telling you, our positions could be easily reversed.

Take solace in that.

Come along on this journey. Live a life of truth. Release your pain. Imagine that you have a choice. Suspend your disbelief. Consider that your burden could be lighter, even if the details of your life remain exactly the same. Stop tolerating discontent, misery, helplessness, resignation. Let go of the giving up. If you can't do it for you, start by doing it for me. It won't be long before you are doing it for both of us.

For the rest of this book, (and perhaps for your forever, if you will invite me to be) I am your therapist. I am in it with you. I know that I can't be in the room with you, but I hope that my spirit and energy can remain as you read this book and long after you put it down. If you don't believe that this is possible, give me a chance to prove it. When I ask you to be thoughtful about something, consider that the life you save is your own. When I ask you to tell me your darkest most raw primitive truths, realize that you are most importantly speaking to yourself. No one else needs to hear. But you do.

The life you save is your own. (Did I say that already?) The world will not come crashing down. You will not drown.

You will breathe.

Don't be afraid. I will help you.

# CHAPTER 1

# A Few Things (I Need to Tell you Before Anything Else.)

"I don't give them hell.  I just tell the
truth and they think it's hell."
HARRY TRUMAN

I have a client (still do) who came into my office several years ago for couples therapy with her (then) husband. At first glance she was somewhat daunting to me. She was 15 years my senior, very well-spoken, obviously well-educated and seriously employed.

Our first couples session was pretty standard. She and her husband each expressed, with the usual mixture of controlled rage and faux polite apology ("No offense, but...") their specific sides of the story complete with the dreaded, *and everybody thinks so!* which is so often called upon in such situations. It doesn't matter if you are 16 or 60; everyone has the propensity to be 16 when they sit down to do couples.

First and foremost, I felt for them. Couples therapy sucks. Even if you're the happiest couple ever to have entered into couples therapy, it still sucks. There you are, beside this person with whom (oftentimes) you feel inextricably tied, airing your most embarrassing and revealing stuff to a virtual stranger. I have facilitated couples therapy for years, and I have occupied the hot-seat myself. I am here to tell you that I feel for you too, if you've braved these waters. It's really hard.

So, I did what I do. I listened attentively and actively, allowing both of them to have their fair share of stage. I allowed them the freedom to, perhaps for the first time in a long while, feel heard without the panic that they would be interrupted and undercut at any moment. I responded with a word or two as appropriate, so each of them knew that I was totally hearing. Not just listening, but hearing.

Once I felt that each had adequately vented, I broke the (what I've found to be) somewhat surprising news:

"I am not the judge and jury, guys. I am here to mediate, and listen, and care about each of you, but you don't need to argue your cases to me. You don't need to prove to me with the text messages on your phones that you know you are right," I apologized. "I am really here to help you to uncover what you are actually arguing about."

My statement was met with confused silence. This is normal.

Most people don't know quite what to do with this information, initially. Obviously they know what they are arguing about! For God's Sake, it happens every day. It's the "tone she takes with me," or the "way he always leaves the screen door open, even though I've told him a thousand times how much it bothers me!"

In our work together, each of these human beings will come to understand one of the greatest mantras of my practice: If there are underlying unresolved issues in a relationship, everything from the moment you wake up to the moment you go to sleep, is fodder for an argument. Everything.

In the case of the couple at hand, as I always do, I advised them that I wanted one individual session with each of them to attain a full picture of the situation without the hesitation attached to sitting beside one's partner. I've never met with opposition to this. People need, in fact they are dying to express themselves without the limits set by their own fears. I feel them, and I consistently give them this option.

Over the years, I have observed that regardless of our cultural norms or a couple's final decision to stay together or split up, everyone needs freedom of expression along the way. In fact, I have found that many couples who might have ultimately ended their relationships (in my prediction) had we not stumbled upon one another in this crazy life, have been able to turn things around within this safety - this freedom to speak their truths without fear. When people finally feel heard, they are able to stop defending every point, every time. The freedom I am discussing is exactly what I offered my client and her husband, at the conclusion of our first session.

She scheduled her individual appointment right away, for the beginning of the following week. This woman blew into my office like wildfire, seating herself decisively on my opposite couch, and planting her massive designer handbag squarely next to her. She looked directly at me for a moment. Then she said,

"I think my husband is cheating on me."

I was like, "OK... let's talk about it." After all, I'm not *that* psychic. I didn't have a clue, at the moment, if he was or wasn't.

She chose to tell me, first, about the beautiful beginnings of their relationship 15 years prior. She recounted their wedding as the best day of her life. She told me that on their first date after hearing a portion of her story he had praised her as being the strongest woman he'd ever met. She cried bitterly as she compared the ways in which her current life differed from these lovely memories.

I sat there. I listened. I watched her beautiful humanity take shape within my four walls, far sooner than I'd expected it might. I observed her bravery, as she allowed herself to be raw and vulnerable. Personally, I struggled with the perceived power differential. She was a force to be reckoned with. I was (in my mind at the time) a younger therapist who should, potentially, watch her step in order not to offend. I waited as long as humanly (Nicole-ly) possible, before blurting out,

"I have a question."

I wasn't sure if a therapist had ever interrupted her before to actually ask a question during a heated monologue, because she seemed rather surprised, but at the same time curious and willing. She looked up from her lap. "Yes?"

"Do you know?" I began, "And maybe you do... but just in case. Do you know that if he is cheating, and if you... happen to feel the need to acknowledge this, and perhaps even to rethink the state of your marriage... that your wedding day can still be the best day of your life?"

Her countenance shifted, just a bit. I saw an opening. A beautiful opening which, over the years, I have learned never to ignore. Not with her, or anyone.

"Do you know that you can still be the strongest woman he (or you) has ever met?" I continued, with renewed confidence. "Do you realize, that when you need to walk away from something, you still retain the beauty that has become, you? He did not give this truth to you, and he cannot take it away. He may have been the fertilizer, but you... you are the flower! It is you. And you are always, *always* still you."

She looked right at me for more than 30 seconds, her face an unlikely but warm combination of shock, sadness and peace.

Then she mumbled, "Oh my God."

It was one of the defining moments in my evolution as a therapist, giving me the confidence to interrupt a person's well-tread dialogue to invite in the truth that heals. You should see her now.

~ঽ

This book is basically about three things (in any order, and all at once): Trust, Courage and Truth.

The problem with using these words to describe this book is that the typical human does not define any of them the way it is necessary to really get what I am saying and, in turn, change his or her life. Our whole lives we have been taught that if you are unclear of a definition, look it up in the dictionary! And we have, time and time again. We have understood the meanings, or so we thought.

We build entire lives based on these definitions. We convince ourselves so effectively that we know who we are, or what it means to be "happy," or "tired," or "successful," or "angry," or "inspired," or "disappointed," or (the most damaging if you ask me) "right."

I am here to challenge our definitions, of a lot of things. I am not here to be a rebel, or a hero. I am challenging our definitions because I have learned the most incredible secret that many of us know on some level, but so few of us are able to access enough to heal. I have uncovered this gem, first and foremost, through a battle with myself that has been both excruciatingly painful and bizarrely healing. And then through years of working therapeutically with many clients. I've learned to stop listening to the dictionary. And it has created my life.

I have watched as people have literally lit up (ignited!) with the shock of epiphany. I have seen people who were trapped and stuck and hopeless take back their power, incredibly. I have witnessed people evolve from crippling chronic pain and "incurable" conditions first to tentative hope, and then finally to the kind of realizations that have assured me they will not be fooled again. (Pls. indulge *The Who* reference. It was my first real rock concert in high school and it sticks with me.)

But no shit; I have seen all of these things. Many times. Plus (a major plus,) I have witnessed my own transformation. And I'm not scared to tell you all about it, if you will accept that gift.

Not the normal therapist, huh?  Willing to reveal details of my own life?  Willing to use myself to help you understand?  Unafraid to show you my humanity, my weaknesses?  Well yeah, I am willing to do that, even though my traditional psychodynamic training is skeptical about this kind of sharing.  I am brave enough to pull a Lewis and Clark here for two reasons, the more significant of which has been shown to me too many times to ignore: If I am not a human being in the room, with you and for you, you cannot heal.

If I don't do this, maybe you will heal a little bit.  But a little bit's not good enough for me.  The other reason is simple.  An amazing professor in grad school, Dr. Mari Ann Graham, showed our class *Good Will Hunting* as an educational tool and explained to us how "self-disclosure" can change a client's life.  I heard that, Mari Ann.  I haven't forgotten.

I have learned with passionate certainty (if you choose to believe me just long enough to take my hand and come along,) that there is literally one way to achieve actual freedom from your damage or your patterns, or whatever you personally call *that trapped feeling* that sneaks into your thoughts regardless of your best efforts to ignore it.

This way is truth.

But remember, your definition of the word will not work.  Give me a chance to explain it better.  Open yourself, my friend.  The life you save is your own.  I said it again.  I did that.

I invite you to come along, or… don't.

I say this not to be negative, but mostly because I'm aware that if I boss you around, you will simply rebel.  It's human nature, and you are a human person.  I can't help you if you sit, arms crossed like a defiant teenager, justifying the reasons that your specific brand of pain or conflict cannot be touched by my words. So, I give you the choice. I offer you this power. *You will need it, because personal power protects us from our own resistance.* As you begin to consider that it might be helpful to look into [my definition] of [your] truth, you may be gripped by a passionate yet curious rebellion against feeling anything this deeply. You may feel angry, or at the very least, defensive.

Perhaps you will huff, "This may be the way for you or your messed-up clients, but it's just not for me!" This is a normal reaction. As we become even vaguely aware of our deeper truths, and they feel ugly, or shameful, or dark, or (the ultimate fear) impossible to access, our natural reaction is to run in the other direction. However, before you flee screaming, please hear this enormous comfort: Your truths can only appear this frightening and blocked, until...

(Try to listen to the next part SO carefully.)

Until they are unmasked, and revealed. Then, and only then, does each of us gain the ability to see ourselves completely. To stop using every ounce of our energy to fight against feeling "bad" or "defensive" or "wrong" or "ashamed." To actually take in what has happened, or not happened. To allow our stories to play out before us in a different, empathic and safe light. Raw pain may accompany this witnessing, but I have watched countless times as people have smiled through tears because they have also been able to see the beauty. The beauty of truth without judgment is striking, as it is only through this lens that we can be forgiven. You can be forgiven. And it's such a relief. We all, simply, just want to be forgiven.

Even so, you may convince yourself that you don't need to feel anything new, different or disturbing. Once again, this is a normal defense mechanism, and we need to put that rebellion somewhere. We certainly don't want that tantrum (i.e. your brain's rage and resistance) to turn inward and make you feel frustrated and angry at yourself! This will do us no good. It will only fortify your pain and inner conflict. So if you feel yourself getting annoyed, or angry, or God forbid apathetic, I have an idea:

Be mad at me! Seriously. Feel free to tell me to fuck off any time you choose while you read this book. I can take it.

But keep reading.

~⁓

As I write this, I'm listening to a singer/songwriter named Ron Pope. For the first time, ever. And out of nowhere he sings,

"All of our heartfelt lies......are not enough this time."

Wow. Talk about the universe singing to us! That's the exact point of the moment. Your moment! You are sitting there reading this because you are hurting, maybe badly. You want more from life. You want to understand why you feel and do things; you want to stop your pain and stop being afraid. You want to feel better. Listen to this voice that is speaking to us. Maybe it is yours, or mine, or Ron Pope's, or some combination. It doesn't matter. The most important point is that your true voice doesn't lie to you, if you are willing to listen with gentle curiosity and openness to possibilities. I'm here to free up some space within you, so you can hear it.

If you were my client sitting in my office, feeling my support and genuine dedication to your growth, you would soon say, "I feel it, Nicole. I'm starting to understand." And you wouldn't be saying it for me. It would be for you. This has a lot to do with our earned trust, and the fact that you are starting to see yourself. I know I can't do this personally for each of you, yet we can try to cultivate that trust here, in this book. As we work through this important process together, I have only one request. I'm going to ask you to suspend your disbelief.

I'm going to ask you to consider that a *psychological process might affect a physical condition.* Even if there is a debating society in your head regarding this concept, I'm going to ask you to pause it with the following question you must ask to yourself: "How long would you like to suffer?"

If the society screams that there is no way this could work for everyone, I ask you to consider that this may be true. But I think it can work for you.

There is no need to believe solidly that this is possible right now. I ask only for your willingness to embrace a new idea. This new idea will ultimately hand you back your entire life. How about, let's pretend it is the end of the world, and I have the last remaining seed for the only fruit-bearing tree. (Am I being too dramatic? Probably. My apologies, but I just know that life is so much harder if you don't at least try to get this.) Just sit with me until the tree grows and sprouts fruit. Then, even if you are still skeptical, you can take a bunch in your basket and walk away. No hard feelings.

~

We need to discuss your brain. I said those things earlier about your defiance and anger because you don't yet know consciously how compelled you will be to hide from your truth. Insisting that I don't know what I'm talking about is the quickest way for your brain to settle back into the pattern of your chosen brand of diversion, or self-destruction. Oftentimes this diversion comes in the form of physical pain or conditions. Pain is an excellent distractor, as it demands your immediate and often constant attention. Plus, it is falsely empowering in that it allows you to feel as if you are "in action" as you go from doctor to doctor, or treatment to treatment. Sadly, it is also bizarrely comforting, as people in pain get other people to pay attention to them. As human beings, we seek to connect in any way that we can, and being in pain and requiring care and concern is one way to achieve that. However, if you are reading this I'll bet that the payoff is wearing thin for you. You need and want connection, but you're starting to understand that there has to be a better way to achieve this. You can't stand hurting like this for one more day. I hear you.

Sometimes we divert ourselves with self-destructive habits. Over-drinking, drug use, smoking cigarettes, helping everyone else with their problems all the time in order to not focus on our own, eating things that we know will make us feel like crap, or deciding not to eat at all, etc. Whichever poisons you pick, these personal security blankets of self-torture are diverting your attention, and they are doing an awesome job.

Remember... all the while you are obsessing on being "right" or "fat" or "unable" or "less than" or even "in pain," you are protected from thinking about the darkest, most seemingly unreasonable truths that live within you whether you acknowledge them or not. Essentially, you are protecting yourself by the way you think and behave, as if the truth will end you, but I gotta tell you. (Brace yourself.)

The Truth Shall Set You Free.

Although I'm aware that this statement originated in the Bible and was initially meant and taken very seriously, it has become quite cliché over the years, as it's been used in everything from cartoons to TV commercials. Hence, I feel my father turning in his grave as I write this; he was the cliché-hater extraordinaire. Even so, phrases which have become cliché are cliché for a reason - universally, enough people in history have acknowledged their power. Although I fully acknowledge the cheese factor that this statement has somehow adopted, it's so important for you to embrace if you want to leave all of the festering negativity in your life behind.

You have an opening in your journey to choose a different way of looking at the world. No matter how challenging, if you undertake this personal excavation I promise you it will be the greatest gift you have ever given yourself. You can literally heal yourself of your pain. There is more waiting for you, in your specific life. And how could I possibly know? Because I have seen you. All of you...in my office.

You say, "It wasn't me."

I say, "It was."

The sooner you realize that we are all the same (Young Old Rich Poor Left Right Gay Straight Black White Purple) in our most basic essence, the sooner you stand to take back your own life. Why? Because all of a sudden you have become less alone than ever. Our organic need to be connected to other people is innate, and powerful. Knowing that other people are "in it" with us is often the determining factor in overcoming unthinkable challenges. You are the same as everyone else who is in pain, at the moment you are in pain. Knowing this can help you save your own life. The human race is a lovely warm bunch of people, and you were born with a membership card. Membership has its privileges.

I am inviting you to sign up for something difficult. It's way harder, initially, than taking a pill, or having a needle inserted into your back, or spending 3 days a week at the physical therapist. I'm not trying to be melodramatic, and I certainly don't want to deter you. I'm saying this for two reasons: One, your brain will fight you. As I said, it thinks it is protecting you with the pain as a diversion from your dark truths. Two, as a member of the human race you are a victim of the ugliest concept in the English language next to *right*:

Expectations.

William Shakespeare put it perfectly when he said, "Expectation is the root of all heartache." I'm so with him. Expectations kill us, every day of our lives. You know why? Because nothing is ever as we expect. Literally. Regardless of what you think you expect from your marriage, or your job, or being a child of someone's, or being a parent yourself, or being a friend, or (and this one is huge) being *you*, you are always mildly to absolutely disappointed. Maybe you are crushed. Society has poisoned us with fairytale expectations that were super fun when we were five and planning to grow up to be pop-stars, but as we've aged they've gently murdered us.

And guess what? The most mild ones are the most damaging. Even though I don't think that my 8-year-old daughter really believes she's going to be Taylor Swift one day, she absolutely thinks that certain definitions hold fast and true, and they are brewing in her growing little mind like the darkest roast Starbucks Coffee. Concepts like "love," "motherhood," "career," "marriage," "friendship," "success," "happiness," "beauty..."

I can't do much to help her, yet. I certainly will not be able to shield her completely. I have accepted that. She will have to live her life, and live her decisions. I will however, relentlessly, do the only thing I can do to protect her - I will be constant in my passion to continually uncover my own truths so I don't unconsciously cause her any pain that is truly, mine. I see everywhere the way we hurt our children, one another, and ourselves based on our unwillingness or inability to look at our personal truths. It pains me to watch this kind of needless suffering. Prove me wrong. Tell me that I'm not alone. Give this precious gift to yourself and ultimately your children, if you choose to have them. Trust me. The payoff is beyond your wildest dreams.

In considering the fallout left in the wake of a lifetime of expectations, you might ponder the question: Doesn't experiencing a bad divorce, or a bankruptcy, or an untimely death, or abuse and neglect, etc. wash these expectations away? People who have lived through any of these harsh realities should be wise to them as a result, right? Quite the opposite actually, kid.

Often a less than idyllic childhood can cause you to hold even more tightly to these perceived expectations, in place of the security you wished to have had. Most likely, you don't allow yourself to be wholly aware of how devastating it is that many of your most cherished expectations fall short.

"How dark and negative!" (You might accuse.) "Why not just look on the bright side, or allow time to heal all wounds, or use good old positive thinking? C'mon!" you beg, "Remember *I'm OK, You're OK?*"

If you grew up around a hippie mom like I did, maybe you do remember that book, and maybe no matter how you were raised, these phrases bring you comfort. But I'm here to say (to shout) you are *not OK!* At least, not until you are. And the path to that place of peace is very different than most people think. And by the way, it's never about getting your way or being right. Never. If you can lay down your weapon long enough to open yourself to what I am explaining, you can absolutely have the tools to change every facet of this useless thinking that has kept you, as I like to say, safe in the unsafest way. I can show you the way to peace.

And you want it. I know this.

That is the greatest truth. I don't care who you are. No one wants to be resigned. Any excuse you could hand me, I would shoot down. I'm… "comfortable," "safe," "trapped," "scared," "unable," "damaged," "clueless," "powerless," "fine!"… That's bullshit. Sorry, it just is. I know you can convince yourself that *It's all good*. Or maybe you go with, "It's not all good, but it's all I can ever have." If you have read this far, there is something in you that is itching to challenge these longstanding truths.

Go further.

# CHAPTER 2

# Me

"I'm nobody!  Who are you?
Are you nobody, too?
Then there's a pair of us - don't tell!"
EMILY DICKINSON
*I'm Nobody, Who are you?*

We are in this together. You and me.

You want help. Help in leaving the pain in your life behind, and creating the future that you know is possible for you. I want to be the one to help you. Here we are.

I have been very thoughtful about how to earn your trust, as nothing real happens without trust. The reason I am dedicating a whole chapter about the *me* in *us* is a direct result of my clients' profound personal growth and resulting overwhelming appreciation, which have been too consistent to ignore. I have worked with people from all walks of life, and although it makes me a tad uncomfortable to share this, I feel like I need to. For you.

The following statements are not exaggerated, not even a little bit. I am sharing them because I know that people like to feel like they're getting something good for their time and money - I know I do. I think the chances of this whole book thing mattering increase a zillion fold if you can believe in me, and you can't believe in me if you have no good reason to do so. I will take the risk of sounding too proud (my issue not yours,) and tell you this:

I have a full book of appointments. This means that my practice is full. I work as much as possible for a mother of 5 who actually wants to parent her kids. When I sit across from my clients, I am completely present, alive, attuned, and dedicated to their growth and healing. I am unafraid to be personally vulnerable, and/or revealing in concert with their needs. I am a human being right there with them. Every single client with whom I have worked has told me the same thing: "Therapy has never sincerely changed my life, until I worked with you."

Every single one.

I light up. I glow when I hear that statement, every time. It never gets old and it never feels less powerful. I bask in the light that my clients emit as they grow and change; as they feel pride in themselves. I need you to know this about me and about us, because I am offering you the same gift. I have written this unique book for you. It is for you, and for me, and for every client who blinks back tears and writes me cards, and offers me their first-born children (ugh... no thanks, I have 5) out of appreciation.

Would an example help? OK, let's. Let me tell you a bit about my practice, and my life. I think you will hear me much more clearly if you know me a little more. The concept of *knowing* is so often overlooked in therapeutic partnerships. Clients are expected to walk into a total stranger's space, plant themselves down on a moderately uncomfortable sofa, and spill their guts without the vaguest notion of the person who sits before them. Trust me, I've been there. After my father died suddenly when I was 27, and my entire world was rocked as I (not only) had to fly the red-eye to London to arrange for his burial (alone) but (also) return to the States to dismantle his entire life, I decided it might be a good idea to find a therapist!

Her name was Diane, and she was perfectly nice. She was warm and kind, and I felt pretty comfortable with her in general. But I remember having the strangest feeling every time I allowed myself to be even slightly vulnerable in her presence. I felt small, and weak, and less than. I felt alone. This seemed odd to me, since she was really thoughtful and attentive. Yet somehow these feelings gripped me, time and time again. I couldn't push away the notion that she was strong and wise, and I was defective. I allowed myself to be convinced that this was simply what therapy was all about. I had to accept this dynamic if I wanted to be helped. Here's the thing, though.

As kind as she was... she didn't really help me.

As I have grown as a clinician and cultivated the theories which have come together to create this book, it has become clear to me what I had needed all those years ago, the missing piece. One of my first clients in private practice, Brooke, told me early on in our work that she had been to therapy for various reasons throughout her life, and this was the first time she really felt connected, and able to heal. I was like, "Really? Thank you! But might I ask... why?" And you know what she said? I will tell you.

She said, "Because you told me you had kids."

Now, you might be sitting there and saying, "So what? So you have kids? That doesn't exactly make you the best therapist to have ever drawn breath."

Perhaps. Yet, for my Brooke sitting there feeling scared and para-lyzed and stuck in her life, and unable to parent her difficult young girls the way she wanted and needed to, it changed everything. I became more than just a random therapist witnessing her embarrassing damage with no clue how it might feel. I became a human, a peer, another mom in it with her, fighting the good fight. She could exhale. She could, at her pace and with my warm support, locate the truths that she needed in order to embrace her life. She was not alone.

Before you freak out, please note that not every client of mine is a mom, or a woman, or an only child (or any number of other labels which would apply to me, personally.) Yet, I learned an essential les-son that day from Brooke, which has stayed with me. I learned that therapy cannot be about a needy person seeking Godly wisdom from a perceived perfect being. It must be two humans sharing their humanity.

That is, as long as the therapist's every effort is focused in the precise direction of the client's needs. I am continually vigilant to make sure that regardless of the part that my humanity might play in the therapeutic process, it is never about me, or about solving any personal issue on my back burner. A therapist can never take this lightly. However, dismissing the imperative human factor in therapy often results in spinning wheels, on a road to nowhere. This is hard to deny when so many people have confirmed it over the years, often without my even thinking to ask.

> AUTHOR'S NOTE: I use the word "humanity" a lot, so it makes sense to take a moment and define it in context. I find humanity to be a beautiful word which, for me, is attached to a feeling of belonging, connection and togetherness. I see one's humanity as her essence, her nature - his or her spirit. I also see it encompassing our flaws and imperfections - all that which makes us human. When I refer to people *sharing their humanity,* I am giving them the highest compliment. I am commenting on the bravery it requires to reveal oneself to another human, to show our lovely imperfections without fear, as in the old expression, "warts and all!"

This kind of sharing frees us so much, regardless of whether we are on the giving or the receiving end. Hopefully you have played both roles and continue to do so, all the time. If not, well, that's why you're here! We're gonna talk all about how to access your humanity, and in turn, your truth. After all, within your truth lies lasting healing.

Moving on! Now we can get to the most important part of our equation: the particular You. I may be integral in this process, but keep in mind that I am never as important as you. I am however, *with* you. That's why you will be able to do this.

Because you are not alone.

I am well versed in the significance of the "not alone." Without getting too deep into my story (as you will be so sick of me once you get through the *JournalSpeak* chapters,) I've spent many years in an effort to keep people as un-alone as humanly possible. I spoke publicly for years to countless patients at NYU Medical Center's Rusk Institute for Rehabilitation Medicine in New York City on the topic of overcoming chronic pain during the years I participated in Dr. John Sarno's Alumni Panel.[1]

At that time I had recently overcome the greatest challenge of my young life: a virtual death sentence handed down when I was only 19 years old. I chose to reveal my raw humanity to lecture halls of people from all walks of life, originally to help and inspire others through the simple act of their witnessing my trauma and triumph. Yet, as I grew as a clinician and evolved as a person, I realized that sharing one's frailties is about much more than witnessing.

Sharing is dynamic. It is the greatest interactive healing tool available to us as people. The most generous thing human beings can do, and the most empowering, is to unabashedly speak their truths (once they have understood them and healed) to others.

The most basic need of human beings is to connect. We connect with others when we give of ourselves without fear. And in turn, we feel connected with others when we realize we are not alone.

Once you begin this profound journey toward your deeper truths, your greatest challenge will be to accept the need (that I am imposing upon you) to defy much that has comforted you, or sustained you, or made you feel normal over your lifetime of living. You have needed your stories and patterns in order to find a way to feel safe. I will help you to understand how this brand of safety can lead to misery. In the

NICOLE J. SACHS, LCSW

mean time, I know that these habits have served you well until now. Don't get all nervous, you can keep them.

For the moment. At the moment, you need them to feel safe.

Let's talk about safe. It is essential to feel safe. There is nothing without safety. No growth, no change, no healing, no nothing. Except pain. It's the same as the old adage, "Without your health, you have nothing." Well, yeah. Because if you are fighting constant pain, or paralyzing fear, or debilitating depression, or actual impending death, there is no room for hearing anything about anything else. That's just the way it is. I can't imagine anyone could argue with that one.

But you are not dying. You might feel like you are sometimes, but you're not. So you and I need to evolve a deeper, truer safe. We can do it together, if you provide the bravery. I will take care of the warmth and wisdom. I tend to say that we are all innocent liars. There is no direct malice in these lies that we tell, to ourselves or others. In fact, there is a good chance that we keep the truth from ourselves as vehemently as we do from the world. We protect ourselves by being certain of "what happened," or "who we are," or "what we could handle." Yet, if you can listen for a moment without defense (remember - no one can see you,) I have something that you need to hear:

You decided to buy this book.

I have no idea why. But I don't matter, in this case. You do. You heard something or thought something, or some meddling friend was like, "You need to read this book, it could help you." Or whatever the hell. For a reason, you are reading this. So, you may as well pay attention. Right? You know why something about this made you take notice. And you are important...you are everything. You hold the key to every jail in which you sit, and we all inhabit several all at once. Just trust me, your dollars have been well spent.

As you will see in the *JournalSpeak* chapters the truths I have uncovered, and continue to uncover within myself have, quite literally, handed me back my life. How can I be more profound? Ok, let's try. They have created my entire happiness. (Fine, happiness is not a permanent state of being.)

How about: They have cultivated my peace.

That, I will stand by. Only within personal peace can a person even consider his or her definition of happiness. I may not spend my life dancing in figure-eights surrounded by sunshine and vocal Disney creatures, but I am warm and content. I experience many moments of pure joy, and I have few if any regrets. Most significantly, I feel as if I have narrowly escaped a life of resignation and conflict. Happiness is not a permanent state of being; *happiness exists in moments.* It is a by-product of the kind of freedom which needs only exist in the mind, and spirit.

This freedom is only possible through truth.

Keep in mind that I am still on this journey. Always will be, just like you. I, myself, have oftentimes reflected on those periods of my life when I've needed to do extraordinary things - for my kids, or myself, or my parents - and had no earthly idea how I came up with the strength. Yet, as I work passionately with the brave people I call clients, I have started to really get it. And here is it:

As a result of uncovering and accepting many of my own deepest truths, I have begun to learn who I actually am. Not the bullshit story of me I had created and bitched about to my friends endlessly over the years. Not the *shoulds* I'd embodied as spoken by my parents, or the mean girl at school, or the seemingly disapproving world. Not the self-imposed guilt perpetuated by misunderstood religion and culture. I have learned to introduce myself, to me. It is the most freeing process I have ever experienced. As a result, I now know what I think about things.

I'm not scared of being vulnerable, or raw, or seen. I'm not offended if you choose to disagree with me. I don't need everyone to like me. I am comfortable being different, if that's what feels right, depending on the situation. I can still breathe if I'm not perfect. Most importantly, I have come to like who I am, without arrogance. A huge part of this unlikely combination is cultivated because I always share my humanity with whomever is before me. So no matter how much I may like myself, I remain human and flawed. Because I am, as you are. I can admit to you my shameful failings. I can forgive myself right in front of you and then, tell you how I did it. I can say things that shock you in their honesty, about myself. And then, somehow, magically... you can say your things to me. Because we are together, in it.

Can you feel what a big deal this is? This is such a big deal. Check in with yourself to assess whether or not you feel it - if you get this. If you come up with a moderate to strong yet honest, "No," I propose that we be gently curious about the possibility that...

Just perhaps.

You are so deeply entrenched into your personal situation that you can't even conceive that your life is in need of such a close look. Or you think, "Maybe it is, but my situation is impossible to change." If this is you, no worries. We can handle that. In truth, we can handle anything. If you are up for it, so am I. I'm not afraid. Just stay with me. I'm here to kindly tell you: I know what you need.

(Insert indignation.) "How can you be so sure? What the hell happened to you as a child? Did your parents constantly make you a winner? Are you one of those Gen X kids who got a trophy at every game, even though the other team obviously won? Did you live your life thinking that nothing you did was anything but brilliant?" Um... totally not, in case you were really wondering. Quite the opposite. That is likely the reason you are sitting here with me, reading my words. In any case, your point is well taken: Why on earth should you listen to me? You, my dear, hold the answer to that one.

Let's look at your life, together:

Is physical pain owning your life? Are you aching all over? Are you hurting in one specific place, and then just when you feel some relief, in another place? Think carefully because sometimes this process is tricky, but I'll bet you that it's happening. Do you have a diagnosis that has no known cure, only treatment? Do you, in your private thoughts, question whether or not that diagnosis can even account for your symptoms? Do you spend your days being frightened that you won't be able to live a full life as a result of your state of health?

Or maybe your marriage is in ICU, although you know somewhere in there that the main roadblock is you? Are you the one who has cheated, but you hide from that wildly? Has your partner cheated or left, yet you have no real certainty where it went wrong? Do you need something that you can't define? Are you in emotional pain? Stuck? Depressed or anxious, but not desperate enough to seek real help? Alone, in any sense of the definition, even in a crowded room?

Maybe you try so hard to feel fulfilled, and it seems as if nothing makes a profound difference. Your partner seems distant because he or she doesn't *understand* you. You feel as if you don't understand you. Your mother doesn't get it. Or, in your gut, you know it's your mother who has hurt you the worst, but that's not polite to discuss. It makes you feel embarrassed and alone. Perhaps your best friend was cool and seemed to want to hear about your life up until a point, and now she's had enough. She really doesn't want to listen to your crap, you can tell. It makes you feel so rejected.

Maybe you really wanted kids so much and you couldn't live without them, but this whole parenting gig is not what you expected. You need so badly to be a good parent. Yet, in truth, you aren't even exactly sure what that means or how to do it "right." You feel empty a lot. Everything is exhausting. You're not enjoying life as you should, and it's going by too fast. You feel guilty sometimes, and you don't even know why.

Or...

"Actually Nicole, I know exactly why. Yeah, um, but that doesn't feel better either. Because there is no changing it."

Not to worry if I didn't name you above. I could, if I had a session alone with you. Either way, don't stress it my friend.

In truth, the specific details of your life don't matter so much. What does matter is your desire for more openness to possibilities, presence in the moment, appreciation of your blessings, and ability to live comfortably without the emotional and physical pain you can't shake.

They say, "Look before you leap!" Right? Well, in your journey toward deeper truth, this adage is crucial, just with a little twist. Before you leap, you must be seen.

# CHAPTER 3

# I See You

"I.... s e e....y o u...."

JAMES CAMERON

*Avatar*

Have you heard of the movie *Avatar* by James Cameron? If not, I would love to see the rock under which you live. It must be remarkable! Ok, just teasing. The reason I am asking you this, is that sometimes the best way to open oneself to a difficult or painful concept is to, for the moment, lighten it up. This is heavy stuff that we are talking about, and I want you to be able to relax and listen. In addition, I think those massive blue Avatar people make my point really well. Don't worry if you haven't seen it - you'll still get it. No purchase necessary. Let's do it.

Ok. So, you probably think the Avatar quote on the title page of this chapter is corny. It is. Here is why I needed to do it. Because my friend Robin told me that the movie was "a-maz-ing" the night it was up for all those Academy Awards. And I was like, "Really? I don't know if I can do it."

Fast forward a couple years (a couple centuries in my particular existence.) I'm watching Avatar on HBO with a 5-year-old sucking her thumb and laying on my lap, half asleep. We are at the part when the whole Pandora/Avatar world is ending in destruction, and lies are being revealed, and truths of the heart are the only saving grace.

(Please, just indulge me.)

Jake Sully lay dying, as he was really human and ill-equipped to breathe within Pandora's atmosphere. He had lied to all Na'vi (a.k.a "the blue people") as his Army instructed, but as the beauty of the people revealed itself to him, he defected and decided that he wanted to save them. Neytiri (his Na'vi love,) was so angry and betrayed to find out that he was actually a human in disguise. She told him off in a rage, and tearfully raced away.

Yet! (Brace yourself.) As she began to experience his true dedication to her and to her people, she allowed herself to defy the bullshit that her expectations and *shoulds* had ingrained. In doing so, she became open to seeing something very different.

She saw his beauty; his particular truth.

She grabbed the oxygen mask, thrust it onto his human face (which she had never even seen before!) and in the last moment to save his life, she calmly said, "I SEE YOU." He recovered from death (I'm totally acknowledging the cheese factor here, but it's so good) and croaked, "I SEE YOU."

No kissing or typical Hollywood BS. Just that: "I see you." Right there, in that moment I got it: Before we can attain the connectedness which is our lifeblood, human beings need to be seen for their soft, vulnerable, lovely true selves, no matter how flawed. People need to be seen before they can be loved right, or treated right. It is impossible to do right by someone until you know who he or she is in the first place!

This process begins with seeing.

Yet, seeing people isn't easy for other people in their lives with whom they have shared conflict, or even just history. Each human looks at the world through a lens that is created by his or her origins, and is then shaped further by his or her upbringing. In addition, once we live some part of our lives together, we humans take our buried insecurities and anger and assorted issues, and spread them all over the lens we just spoke about. Through this muddied lens, it is really hard to see one another clearly. I can help you with this. I can help you because I understand that in order for them to heal and grow, people need to be seen, despite _____.

Despite... You must help me out here now and fill in your human-ity - your damage, your fears, your defenses; your history. There is nothing you could say that would cause me to judge you. Nothing. You are simply a member of the human race, and we all react to the same crap with the same shit (pun intended.) Once I know what you've got there in your closet, I can sort it out and teach you how to see your-self. The reason I am able to do this in the first place is because I am able to see you, any of you. I see you, regardless of all the muck built up on the lens through which you look, in order to see yourself and the rest of your world.

Having said all of this, I propose, gently...

# CHAPTER 4

# the Truth
# (part I)

> "I remember someone old once said to me
> that lies will lock you up, with truth the only key.
> But I was comfortable and warm inside my shell,
> and couldn't see this place could soon become my hell."
>
> MISSY HIGGINS
> *The Special Two*

Y ou need something that you don't know you need.

You are in my office, so you know you need something. Guidance, maybe? Resolution of a particular conflict in your life? Support during a difficult time? Perhaps there is an issue with your partner? Maybe you feel anxious, depressed, searching, miserable, confused, hopeless, stuck? I hear you.

Of course, as a person who is even willing to consider therapy as an option, you know you need something.

I can quickly tell, however, that our work together will be more complex than the list of issues which pour forth on our first meeting. Regardless of the presenting problem you bring to me, beneath any discomfort or trauma or confusion in your life, you need one fantastically important thing first: You need to be seen. Then, and only then, can I help you to unearth the salient issues which underly your troubles.

Similar to our Avatar (Na'vi ) friends, I'm obviously not talking about using my eyes to discern your hair color, or the style of your Uggs. I'm talking about looking at *you*, past your intellectualized stories, your justifications and fears, and the excuses that you have told yourself for-ev-er. To kindly and gently see you, and to let you know that I do.

I can then explain to you what I see.

Now, don't get yourself into a panic that I am some weird Svengali (a bit of a Seinfeld reference, for you fans out there) who is going to look deeply into your soul and tell you awful disturbing truths about your hidden inner-being. I mean, I kind of am, but in the nicest possible way. Insert a quiet smile here. C'mon. We need some form of levity or we'll never get through this.

Not to fear. Any truths we uncover will arise from your willingness. There is nothing I can tell you about yourself that you don't know. At the moment, you just don't know that you know. You need willingness and courage, and openness to possibilities. You need permission to invite the embarrassing drunk uncle to the party. Once we have our hands on him, we can actually help him to shut up. Otherwise, you will worry for the rest of your life that he might show up at any significant life event!

Joking aside, there is a method to my madness. There is a reason that my seeing you allows for any and all growth to take place. You need to be seen, truly seen with compassion and kindness and love and forgiveness, in order to grant yourself permission to see yourself. And as I've mentioned, it is only within this space that deep, lasting healing resides. You may have little idea what it means or feels like to be seen. Perhaps it's been quite a while since anyone has seen you, if ever. One thing is for sure, you need someone to pay attention so you can too.

Now. We need to manage your self-judgment. We all judge ourselves so much more harshly than anyone else could, and many times this critical inner voice is the root of our issues. It keeps us from seeing ourselves, for fear of what we'll discover. In order to remedy this, we need to cultivate loads of patience and kindness, for yourself. These essential ingredients take practice to create when they are directed at ourselves, but I can teach you how to do it. They allow for the bravery with which to see yourself, and once you witness the ugliness that is revealed, as every human has in him or her...

You can learn to really forgive.

"I can forgive!" You protest, "I forgive people all the time." Perhaps you do. Perhaps you only think you do. Either way, it is boatloads easier to forgive others than it is to forgive oneself. Forgiveness of self is possible only when we stop defending ourselves and using all of our energy being right. Forgiveness, quite definitively, is born from one concept:

Truth. (The real definition.)

The following is a big reason to perk up your ears.

Each person's story exists on two levels. The first is that which you tell to yourself, or your best friend, or your office mate, or your sister, all the time. You make a phone call, or meet for coffee or drinks and you vent, or unload, or whatever you choose to call it.

I often refer to this as *playing our tapes*. These internalized tapes have been played over and over so much, that many times we don't even realize how we feel about them, at all. Each story, which you throw around over your second glass of wine, or your third cup of coffee, is completely socially acceptable and can be told with almost no emotion. Although these tapes do define the truth for you in some fashion (and they do, according to *Webster's*,) continuing to repeat them will result almost certainly in infinite conflict and pain.

The second level, the deeper truth, is raw. It rarely sounds polite, or socially appropriate. For most of us, the thought of another person hearing these truths even if we could conjure them up would be mortifying, devastating. In your mind, your friends might no longer respect you. Your parents would probably be horrified. Your children would feel unloved and confused. And you yourself, most importantly, would feel as if you were a terrible person undeserving of such self-serving pity and selfish, emotional gluttony.

"You were raised better!" You might say to you. "Suck it up," or "Man up," or "Be the wife (or husband, partner, parent, employee) that is expected of you!"

But here's the rub:

George Berkeley, an 18th Century theologian who is a part of the Western Philosophical Canon along with Descartes ("I Think, Therefore I am") Locke, etc. saw Man's relationship with the universe as one of perception, and manifested through the senses. He proposed, "If a tree falls in the forest, and no one is there to hear it, does it still make a sound?" He wanted to understand our perceptions, and how they guide us in experiencing the world.

I use this question every day to teach you, because you need to know that your perceptions are so powerful. They are your reality, if you allow them to be... which most of us do. If you feel beautiful walking down the street, you are beautiful. If you feel fat by the pool you are fat. If you decide that the decision you made is right, it is right until you decide otherwise. There is no way to ever really know what other people think, even if they'd be willing to tell you. So your perception of yourself is the only reality that you manifest. Your perceptions can lift you or slay you, equally.

In terms of truth, here is what I know about that tree:

It does make a sound, every time it falls, every moment of every day. It falls again and again. And you might not know you hear it, but it makes a sound. It resonates through your entire being. And if you choose not to listen, that is your choice. However, that choice could also mean choosing pain, or depression, or resignation, or despair, or _____. Fill in your blank.

Here is why this philosophical pontification even matters. Whatever your deeper truths might be, hiding somewhere in your subconscious or your intuition, or maybe even fleetingly evident in your conscious thoughts, you *hear* them. You experience them. They are the tree that is falling, constantly. You can pretend they don't exist, but you will always feel them somewhere. They are disguised, as crippling pain anywhere in your body, depression, OCD, anxiety, irritable bowel syndrome, TMJ, stomach ulcers, fibromyalgia, migraines and hundreds of other conditions in this world. These conditions are all real and the symptoms can bring you to your knees, but if you suffer from any of them *just know that I totally think you don't need to.* I'm serious. No matter how "real" something is, there are always several ways to arrive at such a reality, and suppressing one's truth is a pretty damn effective path right on over.

Additionally, and equally as important, I believe that "truth blindness" is the number one reason that people are unhappy in general. It is the culprit behind our communication problems, marital strife, parenting frustration, relationship failure, and personal paralysis. The plague of this condition is so far-reaching, I cannot even fully conceive of it. Yet, my certainty of this fact is so profound that I will tirelessly help you to understand.

I hate to sound like a science-fiction-fantasy-novel-turned-movie, but... This quest will take much courage.

Why? Because of exactly what I keep pounding on. Our deeper truths sound so unpleasant at first and can frighten us so much subconsciously that we spend our whole lives fighting to think about anything else. Our brains serve as excellent partners in crime. They artfully craft many other acceptable diversions, (i.e. your crippling inability to make decisions, your hip pain that won't go away despite every conceivable test or therapy, your body-image issues and disorders, your addictions, your obsessive worry about your daughter's life, your need to be a workaholic, the way you hold onto that boyfriend/girlfriend even though s(he) has proven repeatedly that (s)he isn't right for you.) Etc. Etc. Etc. Blah. This fight for diversion is so exhausting. No wonder you are always tired!

We all do it. We compile our tapes, and we play them, for years. Forever, if we let ourselves.

In the world of our tapes we think we are safe, kind of. We rarely have to see ourselves, look at our weaknesses, or feel (without relentless justification) our roles in each of our personal failures. Yet, there is no escaping the fact that we feel it somewhere. When you moan about your personal grievances, your best friend might suggest, "Well, maybe there's a pill for that." "Or a homeopathic therapy." "Or a self-help book." [Shut up.]

Perhaps you have tried one, or all of these. Yet even so, it seems that none of these factors are making you feel better enough. Even if you are better off than before, or you experience temporary relief, the pain or discomfort moves somewhere else in your body or mind. You don't seem to be able to connect with the deepest issues in your life. You don't feel whole; you know something is missing. Perhaps you are hurting enough that you are ready to try something totally different, anything!

If the mere thought of unearthing your deeper truths leaves you feeling cautious, or scared, or unsure, that's perfectly okay. Remember to take solace in the best, most amazing, life-changing, uplifting part! I can't emphasize this enough, for without this major point there would be no reason to torture oneself with all this hard work: *These (your) deepest (even shameful) truths, once seen felt and gently forgiven, are robbed of their power.* They cannot hurt you anymore, and neither can the emotional or physical ailments that once ruled you. You will no longer need all of your self-destructive diversions.

You will have the power to heal and improve your relationships. You will have the power to unstick yourself from the place in which you've been stuck for so long. If you have the ability and bravery to acknowledge that you need to make even a minor change in your life, the process will be easier than you could've ever imagined. Why? Because change flows like a peaceful river once a person can see him/herself. The seeing becomes the doing. You'll see. This is a process which requires faith, bravery and insight. But it can be done. It absolutely can be done.

So, ask yourself the question.

Do you long to be different than you are? Do you want to not eat that potato chip (or bag) when you've promised yourself that today is the day? Do you want to speak up when someone insults you? Do you want to go to bed without guilt - about almost everything, it seems? Do you want to feel proud of yourself? Do you want to experience the joy your life seems to warrant? Do you want to feel connected and understood by your partner? Do you want to *find* a partner without sabotaging yourself? Do you want to stop abusing the one body you've got? Do you want to not smoke that cigarette? Deep down, would you prefer to be told that your excuses are crap? Are you strong for everyone, and silently hating it because you never get to be the one who is taken care of? Do you have everything you've ever wanted, and still you search for some intangible meaning? (I could go on and on, but you get the pic.)

We paralyze ourselves, my friend. We sit within each of our jail cells, with the key in hand. Or at the very least, the key rests nearby, on some table in the room with us. If you have read this far, and if anything I've said has resonated with you, then you apply. I promise. To be honest, no matter who you are, you apply. I hope you are still reading. I am about to show you the route to freedom.

Take a breath, and relax. I know this is heavy stuff. Just try to be consoled once again by this significant truth: No one needs to hear your deep dirty ugly garbage, but you. You will discover that you are pleasantly surprised and relieved when you finally barf it up, as I begrudgingly call it. I hate to puke, so much, but I must summon the thought because it is a really good analogy. When we are ill, so often we sit, and sweat, and lay still, and beg whichever God exists for us that we will be such good little girls and boys if we can just feel better without throwing up. It is the rare person who welcomes vomit. But sometimes, we just need to do it. So we sweat and panic, and then, eventually, eventually, our bodies make the decision. And there we go.

Maybe this isn't you, but it's certainly me. After it's over, I have always thought: "Ugh. I feel so much better. Why? Why did I fight so hard not to do this? That was such uncomfortable, wasted time."

The same feeling is what so many people express after surrendering, and finally allowing their truths to rise and be reckoned. This surrender is part of each person's process, and although it cannot be summoned at will, it is the natural bi-product of truth-hunting. It's just such a relief. Often people are gripped with regret and confusion as to why they waited so long. Yet I, your consummate companion and guardian, sit in defense of them (of you) and say,

"It's OK, baby. You weren't ready. So I guess now you are."

# CHAPTER 5

# the Truth
# (part II)

"If we will be quiet and ready enough, we shall
find compensation in every disappointment."
HENRY DAVID THOREAU

C heck this out:

This morning as I was helping a client who was struggling with one of his buried truths, he became confused and pondered aloud, "So, it's like Buddhism. We must live in suffering?"

I was very thoughtful about this. I don't know enough about Buddhism to comment on the precise accuracy of his interpretation. This doesn't matter in the moment because regardless, it is a good question to get me thinking about how to explain truth in general, to you.

I took a moment to think, and here is what I came up with:

"Ok, let's say that in your thinking, Buddhism asks us to live in suffering. And, on the flip side, society so often seems to ask that we look on the bright side, or allow time to heal all wounds, or tries relentlessly to divide our actions and thoughts into right and wrong. And, let's agree (which we did) that people are found to be more acceptable or okay if they answer "Fine," when asked, "How are you?" That in fact, most of us hide passionately from admitting, especially to ourselves, that we are actually thinking or acting in any way that might be perceived as bad or wrong or dishonest or shameful or even, simply…different.

"Yes." He agreed. Having said that.

Here is truth:

Truth falls gently into the middle of this continuum. Truth asks us to live in what really, actually, unabashedly, is. We need to see the whole picture, without the natural defenses ingrained in us from childhood, and our resulting self-inflicted judgement. We need to wipe our foggy lenses clean, which allows us to make the acquaintance of the true *I* which exists somewhere within *us*. We need to see our part in each of our successes and failings.

Sounds uncomplicated, perhaps. It's really not. (I'm sorry.) Admitting our truths is not easy or comfortable. In fact, it's so challenging and subconsciously terrifying, that most of us spend many wasted years playing our tapes and talking and acting in erroneously self-serving circles in an attempt to actually feel none of them. A major reason that owning our part is so difficult for human people, is that our part is often not ours, solely. In fact, in almost every case, we have been handed our damage from our parents and our history, both of which combine to create the unconscious reasons behind many of our actions. Why, you might wonder, am I continuing to make this process sound so difficult this early in our journey?

Because it is. But it's better than what you've got right now, and I care so damn much that you choose it.

Remember, if I've learned anything, it is to manage your expectations. It bears repeating: Expectations are the biggest killer in our society - in our world. Misguided expectations slay people's spirits every day. *We are toxic with expectations.* Every facet of our lives is infested with them. Regardless of where your personal internalized expectations are rooted (family pressures, friends' influences, absurd truths you created as a child based on upsetting experiences, whatever you define as society,) they live and breathe as the benchmark of your perceived success or failure.

Regardless, I am here to remind you that this is a process, and you will not fail if you are willing to lay down your weapon and stay the course. It's just gonna be hard. Remember, living in a world of expectations is not a hopeless state of being. It's the only world we've got! If you can allow in an openness to insight and a practice of gentle curiosity about your life, then slowly but surely you can rescue yourself. That is, if you really want to change your life.

Back to truth.

We are going to do a little example, so I can really drill this into your heads before you start to poke around in your own darkest rooms. We do examples a lot in my office. I've learned from you that this is what we need when things get heavy. We are all too intimate with our own stories to really hear a message that hits close to home - our own voices scream too loudly in our ears. I can help you through this. Let me tell you a story about someone else. For the purposes of example, I will speak to the ubiquitous *you*. Meaning, the you in all of us. I will speak to the place in you that relates to every human being.

~

You are a new client of mine. We are sitting in my cozy, warmly lit office. I welcome you, and ask you to share with me the reason you have decided to see me, or more specifically, *where you are at*. Although an ungrammatical sentence, this common social work mantra has become synonymous with: what you are feeling, thinking, or experiencing at this point in time without concern about the past or future. At least for now. It helps the you find presence in the moment, so we can begin with the most salient issue. This is so important, as life is full of other people's opinions and judgements that affect everything we think and do. I want to know where *you* are at. In my mind, this really means (and this is said silently in my head, so don't be scared of me):

"Say whatever the hell you feel like saying. I know there are a million people in your life who are barking in your ears, but you are important, and I am here to listen. This is your time. I am on your side. No one matters except you, for the next hour. Take it in. Feel indulged, or... feel unworthy. I don't give a shit, in the nicest possible way. Just get over yourself for a moment, and tell me the truth. You don't have to recount your entire life - start with one small truth. Then, I can help you. I totally promise."

You don't notice my intense thoughts. You are too caught up in you, which is normal. I was the same, when I was you.

You shift around a bit, attempting to appear appropriate and conversational. Depending on who you are and how you were raised, you might be a little cautious, or a lot. Maybe you try to hide this by appearing overly upbeat - you laugh when something is clearly not lighthearted. But, I know you are smart. And I give you some time. Maybe 15 minutes, maybe several sessions, depending on what you've been handed in life. In any case, I can feel into what will allow you to be comfortable, and free. I give you a world of latitude, because you need it.

And I see you.

After your given time, I begin to understand that you would rather be real with me, and I assure you gently that I do not need polite convo. I explain that I am not a member of the jury, looking to pass judgment on anything you could possibly say. I am a human, just as intimidated by my own stuff. Everyone is, if we could just admit it! There is nothing that you could say that would offend me, or cause me to judge you.

Why?

I stand in firm belief that every single human being on earth could be understood, completely, if he or she was simply seen for exactly *what is*. For example, maybe you grew up with a mom who only approved of you if you were thin, or a dad who only embraced your little self if you got straight A's, and were perfect. Maybe it was unbearably hard, and the abuse you sustained was unthinkable. It was sexual. Perhaps there were physical beatings which had to be survived, by you or your loved ones, without anticipation. Maybe you had the kind of parent who seemed totally normal to everyone else, but somehow she always made you feel crazy. I've seen all of this my dear, and much much more. I feel how hard it is. Perhaps you've always seemed okay to everyone who has known you, and you hate it. You are so sick of being so okay for everyone else, and never for you. You are tired.

Regardless of what you may have suffered, we are in this together. All of us, and there are so many of us. Whomever or whatever you are, I am beyond okay with it. I am a vessel of people's flaws and painful stories. Leave it right here, it's okay with me. We are all members of the same team. I've told you this before, but I will tell you again (as you need me to, I have learned.) Black White Purple Old Young Gay Straight Rich Poor Damaged Fine, we are all the same, in our essence.

I will never let you forget that. You will stay warm and safe, if you remember.

~ૐ

As you begin to understand and integrate all of this, you start to slow down. I see your shoulders lower, and your body position shift and relax a bit. You breathe. You are here for a reason; you know you need to tell your stories to someone. Apparently, I am that someone. Let's do it.

You say:

"I am cheating on my husband. I don't know what I'm doing. I don't even know what matters to me anymore. I mean, I know my kids will be fine. Those teenagers, they don't even care what goes on with my husband and me. They are SO self-absorbed. And you know, I'm not even THAT upset about it, (by "it", I mean what I'm doing,) because the truth is that he has been absent for years. He doesn't pay attention to me at all. My friends know me better than he does. I used to care, but I don't even care anymore. I don't know if I want to leave him or not. I don't know what to do."

I hear you, so much.

I hear you because I am on your side, and a member of your team, and a member of the human race. I know that everything you just said was true for you. In the context of our book this means, you weren't lying to me. At all. Remember our friend Ron Pope, "All of our heartfelt lies, are not enough this time." You came into my office and needed to vent, and you said something to me that you might not even say to your best friend. I have mad respect for you. You are not right or wrong, bad or good, honest or dishonest. People might think that you are any one of these things or you may perceive that they do, but I don't subscribe to that.

In my eyes you are trying, and you are hurting. Maybe you are somewhat depressed, and you worry about really falling into that hole because you've been there before. Maybe you are anxious, and having real trouble sleeping. You're probably fighting with your kids. You feel detached from your friends, even though you won't admit it openly. You show up for all the right events and obligations, but you are really gone. And of course, your marriage is failing before your eyes.

You are handing over your time and money for therapy, and you are probably saying to yourself, "I think I just really need to say my messed up stuff out loud to someone." And, yes. I appreciate the value of dumping your crap on someone else's doorstep. My particular step is an excellent one, for sure. To be honest however, my friend, this venting is but a very small part of your real healing.

Sorry to be like that. I just can't bullshit you.

The second and deeper part of every story that each of us carries within us deep down, is the portion that we (well, really our subconscious selves; our petulant brains) are fighting wildly to hide from.[2] Please continue not to worry if this doesn't make sense to you. Most humans don't even know they are doing it! Recall, your brain is very tricky and protective of you. It can convince you of many "truths" that are actually diversions which serve only to disable you.

~

Back to you, the new client. The following is my translation of your earlier statement into that which I have coined, *JournalSpeak: the Language of Deeper Truth*. Once I know you are safe to hear it, I will tell you everything I have seen, gathered, and interpreted. At that point you will be able to listen, without confusion and panic, and (coupled with my love and comfort) sit with all of your sadness, anger and shame. You will be able to see yourself and the situation that you have allowed, regardless of your best intentions. Then, and only then, will you be able to forgive yourself, and heal. Within self-forgiveness, I can help you to finally decide what to do in order to live a fulfilling life, with personal power and peace. You will release your pain. You will live the life that is available to you.

I will now translate your original presenting problem into *JournalSpeak*. In the spirit of comparison, let's reprint our first dialogue here, so the real you doesn't have to flip back.

"I am cheating on my husband. I don't know what I'm doing. I don't even know what matters to me anymore. I mean, I know my kids will be fine. Those teenagers, they don't even care what goes on with my husband and me. They are so self-absorbed. And you know, I'm not even that upset about it, because the truth is that he has been absent for years. He doesn't even pay attention to me at all. My friends know me better than he does. I used to care, but I don't even care anymore. I don't know if I want to leave or not. I don't know what to do…"

Now. Listen as if you can hear a deep inner voice, the voice I am giving you for the moment. I am giving you the gift of truth, insight and personal power, which you will gain as we work. For the moment, just hear the words with me as if we are translating from a completely different language. Because we are. Here we go:

"I am cheating on my husband…

I know exactly what I'm doing. I'm finally, at long last, doing what the hell *I want* to do. That asshole has tried to control me and tell me how to feel since the day I met him, and honestly… I've had it. I am fucking angry.

Why am I so incredibly angry? I can try to fool myself, but I know the truth. I'm angry at myself for being so stupid to think that a person would change completely just because he went from a boyfriend to a husband. I knew who he was when I married him. He showed me all the time! I chose to ignore it. I have no idea why. Yes, I do. No, I don't. Ughhh. I hate myself for this kind of uncertainty. I feel like maybe, I created this? I asked for it? I feel scared when I feel unsure.

Somehow, all of a sudden, I feel angry at my parents, especially my mother. I never say this out loud, but, why did they make so many selfish choices? They created a child who was so desperate for stability and love that she would sacrifice her own self-esteem for what looked good on paper!

I wish I actually had the courage to talk about all of this. I am so insecure. I think I know why I'm so conflicted about everything all the time: I don't even know if I actually remember enough of my childhood to even believe myself."

~

"I am so very sad."

I'm so sad when I think about that girl... that little girl who was me. I'm so sad for that child, who thought she had the answer to the dilemma of a family who made her feel less than. She was so naive. I cry for her innocence. She had such a strong notion that she could repair it all with the perfect family that she had the power to create...when she grew up.

That sweet girl used her idealistic imagination to deny all of the warning signs. My God, she didn't even allow herself to have a clue that any of these truths existed."

"She was me. She is me.

I am a mother and a wife...but this is not what I expected at all! I have no idea what I actually expected, but I do know that it was so freakin' stupid like the old movies I used to watch with my Grandma. My Grandma was nice to me, actually. I remember that. I miss her. Since she passed away, I never allow myself to really think about that. I don't want to feel sadder than I already am.

You know what, though? I'm a grown-up now, and if I am brave enough to speak it, I think I actually know what matters to me. I'm not usually comfortable saying it out loud, but I think I kinda know.

I want a partner to raise kids with, not just a placeholder. I want to be a good Mama, still, even though they don't call me that anymore. I want to be acknowledged! I want to be appreciated. I want to be heard. Inside, I feel like I want to scream, pretty much all the time."

⌇

"I know what I did.

Instead of asking for any of these things in an understandable manner, I just drifted away. I became a cheater, something I swore was beneath me. I can't justify it. I feel like a disgusting failure. I'm sick over it. And you know what's worse?"

"I'm so scared that my kids will be fucked-up forever.

I know they are watching every interaction between my husband and me. They so get it. I'm terrified that they will hate me and become all messed up in the head, like I am. They will end up making blind decisions like I did, out of confused desperation. My parents were so absent in their spirit, and they never seemed to care about what was important to me. I am so ashamed of my weak self. And do you know why? Can I tell you what makes me feel the absolute worst?"

(Of course you can.  Go ahead.)

"I am doing the exact same thing to my beautiful children!

I can see my kids withdrawing from me, and it is killing me inside.  I try to give it away to adolescence, but I know in my heart that it isn't the whole picture.  My little girl who used to talk to me is a stranger now.  I feel like she knows what a terrible person I am.  How could she not?  Yet, how could she, really?  I have no idea.  All I know is that I'm so lost and confused.  I've never been more upset.

My husband's so distant and I hate him for it, but the truth is that I have no idea what he thinks about anything, and I wish I knew.  My secret dream is that he would just want me again. I want those years back, those years when we were married before the kids - even those first few years after my son was born.

I try to talk to my friends, but I'm embarrassed.  I have no idea if they'll get it, or talk behind my back.  So, I downplay most of it.  I think about this stuff all the time; I just don't tell anyone. Can I tell you a secret, though?  I don't really want to leave him.  I just want him to want me.  I want him to love me like he used to.  I want to love me.  I'm worried that I actually don't know how."

This dose of brave insight in one sitting is impossibly rare, and encompasses many people's situations which I have both witnessed, and lived.  Yet, it's an excellent vehicle by which to understand how we must translate the surface version of our tapes, into our deeper truths.  As this brave woman (the you) lowers her defenses and embraces her truth, she is able to unearth the kind of thinking that will lead to knowing herself.

I am right there with her, and she feels it. Our partnership allows her to continue kicking fear and denial in the face, and combatting the poisons that have led her to become so defensive - the same ones which have kept her stuck.

This is not specifically about my support, though. For reals. You need to know this, since I obviously cannot take each of you through this personally. This is about you not being alone. In order to soothe your sweet little soul, just remember: Truth is an amazing companion, even if you aren't in my office. Take it from me. I don't always have another me with whom to do this. I love it when I can come to a deeper truth simply by connecting honestly with myself in a moment of confusion or need. It is a feeling of incredibly powerful, confident peace. True that.

After this first breakthrough of feeling into a deeper truth, you are on the path of your own *Autobiography in 5 Short Chapters.* This incredible poem, given to me in grad school, had a profound impact on my understanding of how to bring people from confusion to clarity. I have used it countless times in my own life, and in those of my clients. Portia Nelson's writing is the simplest, most compelling piece I have ever read in describing the process by which we humans can ultimately heal by living with our eyes wide open, and embracing each of our truths as we are ready. The unfortunate fact is that one's autobiography cannot be rushed. Clients beg me daily to just, "Please speed it up a little?" I wish I could do so, trust me, in my own life as well! My apologies, but without readiness we each simply crawl back into our holes.

"True readiness is everything," my former supervisor in the world of psychotherapy used to espouse all the time. I believe in the weight of this statement as strongly as I believe in anything. Once a human being can begin to see his own truths, he can commence his process with readiness, and live the path to letting go of his stifling baggage. Once this path is bravely forged, each and every paralysis can be seen, felt, heard, forgiven and remedied.

*There's a Hole in My Sidewalk:*
*An Autobiography In Five Short Chapters*

by: Portia Nelson

Chapter I
I walk down the street.
There is a deep hole in the sidewalk.
I fall in.
I am lost... I am helpless.
It isn't my fault.
It takes me forever to find a way out.

Chapter II
I walk down the same street.
There is a deep hole in the sidewalk.
I pretend I don't see it.
I fall in again.
I can't believe I am in the same place, but it isn't my fault.
It still takes a long time to get out.

Chapter III
I walk down the same street.
There is a deep hole in the sidewalk.
I see it is there.
I still fall in... it's a habit.
My eyes are open.
I know where I am.
It is my fault.
I get out immediately.

Chapter IV
I walk down the same street.
There is a deep hole in the sidewalk.
I walk around it.

Chapter V
I walk down another street.

Once we arrive at each beautiful readiness within ourselves as a result of our hard work of excavating truth, the peace is palpable and it is not hard at all to turn the page and begin the next chapter. I promise. I've seen this happen a million times.

So let's get to the meat of it, shall we? Let's stop being polite! Buckle up. It's time to introduce you to the world of *JournalSpeak*.

**CHAPTER 6**

# The Journey to
# JournalSpeak

"There are few nudities so objectionable
as the naked truth."

Agnes Repplier

I have been thinking a lot about how to explain *JournalSpeak* to you without going into this whole, long story. I can't, however, seem to find another way that captures the spirit and power of this message that you must understand. In order for you to heal and evolve, all of my previous blah blah blah needs to come alive for you. It has to have meaning that you can touch, taste and feel. Recall, this book you are reading is not an instruction manual, it is raw humanity. Although I worry that I am boring you with my self-indulgence (my issue not yours,) I can't deny that I know what you need. So here it is.

~

Let me tell you a story...

I'm sure a lot of really pleasant tales begin with this opening. But this story is not light, or amusing. It is both dark and embarrassing, for me. Yet it is also the most triumphant story of my life. I often look back on this stretch of my life and say to myself, "Thank God for the pain." Without the pain, I would not have been desperate. Without desperation, I would not have seen the way to surrender. And without surrender, I would have never found my truth.

My life would have been something, maybe even something good. But it would not have been this life I lead, full of openness, confidence and faith. I'm going to try to tell you this story in a way that expresses the enormity of the impact that *JournalSpeak* has had on my life. I coined this phrase out of sheer need, as it was through this brand of honesty that my life was born. Bear with me - I will do my best to explain how I discovered it.

~

I have had back pain for as long as I remember. Maybe my earliest memory of the discomfort transports me to around ten years old, getting dressed for school on the winter mornings when it was so cold outside of my warm covers. I would crouch near the vent on the floor, trying to pull on my pants and feel the warmth of the blowing heat at the same time. My back hurt. It hurt worse when I stood, and tried to straighten up. It eased and eventually diminished after I got involved in my day, but I remember it clearly. Even after all these years.

I need to say a few things about my childhood in order for you to see where I am going with this. Just keep in mind that much of the self-pity which accompanied me through college and even grad school dissipated substantially as I became a more seasoned therapist. I still hang with my self-pity at times, just not nearly as often as I used to. Everyone has their hard knocks. But if they are yours, they are yours. So here is a quick summary of mine.

My father was a loving, smart, kind-hearted human housed in the body of a defensive, tortured man who had no idea how to deal with his own dissatisfaction in life. This led to difficulties for him, among them never holding a job for more than a couple years at a time. His ego would morph into "Fuck yourself," and bosses don't like that. As jobs and circumstances changed, the result was constant moving and switching schools. My father's discontent also translated into undying criticism of me, his only child. As we all know, the most effective way to redeem oneself from one's inner turmoil is to torture the next generation to ensure they are better than you are. Other related dramas included personal bankruptcy, and screaming and yelling marital discord. You know the kind.

To be honest, the hardest part was that his disapproval was not confined to the way I behaved. He disapproved of the way I thought.

There was nowhere to hide - even my innermost thoughts were tainted. My little girl truth was that I was wrong and flawed, unless I was perfect.

Yet.

We all know that there is no way to be perfect.

Oh, parents. I am endlessly shocked and floored by the ways in which we damage our children without wanting to, especially when we actually ache for quite the opposite. The result of our conflicted confusion is our erratic behavior which leaves kids feeling confused themselves. We cycle between our true intentions, and acting out the misbehaviors that our pasts have created and perpetuated. In my particular world, the most damaging part about my dad was that he also loved me, and showed me all the time. Vehemently.

You may be crinkling your brow in confusion right now. Although it is counterintuitive, the reason that this killed me was that it created the ultimate conflict. I tell clients every day, if you hate something purely or love something purely, you're pretty safe. It's the conflict that kills. Humans have such trouble living in the in-between. Who could blame us? Darwin has always told us that we will, and inherently must, fight endlessly to be safe. The fittest will survive; the strong ones will find the path to safety. [3] The only problem is that in humans, safety is as difficult to define as "right."

$$\sim$$

As I got older and more complex, my back pain got worse. It became a thing. It became something that I *was*. I was a person who had back problems. It was part of being Nicole. I didn't think it was terribly frightening for most of my childhood, nor did I consider the need to investigate it much further at the time. In my eyes, everyone in the world always complained about his or her aching back.

And so it went, for the little me. Until.

Sorority Hell Week, Freshman Year. I am doing all the stupid shit that people do as Freshmen in college who "go Greek," and I am feeling the absolute certainty, in my estimation, that there is no excuse to bow out. Even if you are near death, you show up for the sisters when they call. I mean, right? Obviously. Duh. If I say anything with passion, I say this: It's not my job to discern what is important, and what is not. If it's real to you, it's real. This was as real as it got for the 19-year-old me.

I'm right in the middle of this nonsense, doing nothing particularly physically stressful at the moment, and my back goes out. When I say out I mean, I can't move. What follows is hysterical tears (not usually my thing, certainly not in front of anyone else,) desperation and finally, surrender. I have to leave school and go home. It's almost Christmas break, so I rationalize to myself that it isn't the end of the world - everyone will be home soon. Even so, I know in some intangible way that this experience takes the whole game to the next level.

Clearly, something is seriously wrong with me.

I try to act natural and socialize as friends trickle in, home from their various schools for the break. I remember that when my Nana has back pain, her doctor instructs her do exercises to strengthen her core. I have seen her do them forever, lying on her back, bringing her knee and hugging it to her chest, then the other leg, repeat, repeat. "Ok," I think. "Maybe this is what people have to do to get better."

To be better.

THE MEANING OF TRUTH

A few days later in an attempt to be socially acceptable, I go to my best friend's house to spend some time with girls I haven't seen since the summer. Her parents have a treadmill and a StairMaster in their basement - it was the 80's after all - and a few girls are there working out. I want to just be okay. I want to be fine, like everyone I know. I want to be normal. So, I get on the StairMaster alongside my friends. I notice tension in my back almost immediately; it tightens. I feel it getting worse and worse, quickly. I lose my breath as the tightness morphs into intense pain, which soon becomes unbearable. I hobble off the Master and lay myself on the floor beside it. "I know what I need to do," I say desperately, to myself.

I begin Nana's exercises. I bring each knee to my chest methodically as I almost puke from the pain. I am determined to be okay. Just like everyone else.

Less than five minutes later, I can no longer keep up the charade. I inform my friends that my back's not feeling great, and I need to go home. "I'm totally fine!" I assure them. "No worries! See you tomorrow I'm sure!" I struggle up the stairs holding my breath, and painstakingly drive the 15 minutes home. Breathe in and out. In and out. Swallow hard. Breathe in and out. Pull into the driveway.

Here we arrive at the very moment my life changed, forever. A moment that will never fade for as long as I draw breath, and here it is: I cannot, no matter how I try, get out of the car.

Now, I'm not saying, "It hurts too much," or "I am so weak!" I am telling you that I cannot will my legs to shift around to the left and search for the ground. I repeatedly attempt to throw open the driver's side door as it creaks back on me over and over, but I have no way to steady it open. I can't adjust my body in the seat to help myself, to exit the car as I've done countless times before. I am in the kind of pain that silences you. There is no crying, no complaining. This is pure unadulterated panic. I can't do anything.

After a few minutes of this torture, I just give up. I lean on the horn. My father is home, yet it takes quite a few loud long honks before he peeks out. I only mention the number of times I hit the horn because my fear and humiliation grow with each blast, and in turn so does my pain. The next few moments are foggy, but I know that he literally must twist me out of the car and carry me up the stairs and into the house.

Thus began the true drama of, "my back." Visits with Orthopedic Surgeons, Tylenol 3 with Codeine, X-Rays and MRIs ensue. And the diagnosis? Let me try my best to capture the surgeon, as he loomed over me laying on the exam table, and told a 19-year-old girl the following:

"You have a condition called Spondylolisthesis (spän-də-lō-lis-'thē-səs.) This means that your spine is not aligned properly, dramatically so, at the base of your spine where it meets the sacrum. Several of the vertebra located at the base of the spine (I love how quickly it becomes 'the spine' and not 'your spine' when one is injured, officially replacing a part of one's identity with pathology) have shifted out of the proper position, and are pressing on the bones below them. You have several spinal stress fractures in these vertebrae. It also looks as if one of the vertebra is actually shattered, and replaced with scar tissue."

If that isn't bad enough, here is what follows.

"This is very serious, and you will eventually need major surgery in order to live without lifelong chronic pain. It will be spinal fusion surgery and will require substantial recovery time, including a body cast for several weeks. Once your spine is fused, you will have decreased mobility for life. Since you are so young, we do not recommend the surgery at this time. Keep in mind however, that you will not live out your days without it. Maybe you'll make it to 40?"

"In the mean time, there are several things that you should never do. You should never ride in a car for an elongated period of time. The bouncing motion will worsen your condition. You should lift nothing heavier than 20 pounds, ever. You could launch yourself into another acute pain incident. You should not sleep on your stomach. It will stress the spine, and deteriorate your condition. If you sleep on your back, make sure that your knees are elevated, always. Best to just sleep on your side in the fetal position. Bend with your knees when picking up anything. Never bend from your back. You should do no exercise which involves bouncing. No jogging. No aerobics. You must give up any sport in which you could have a jarring fall, like skiing, rollerblading, or horseback riding." (Um, my three passions.)

Brace yourself. Here is the best:

"It is unlikely that you will be able to carry a baby to term without bed rest for many months. The weight of the baby will be far too much for your back. Having a biological child may not be a good idea. In fact, you shouldn't really be holding babies very much either. It is a decidedly damaging move - too much emphasis on carrying a heavy thing without dropping it."

At this particular point, in order for you to understand the full catastrophic, resonating impact which occurred in my soul, you need to know one very important thing about me. When I was in 3rd grade and my mother asked me what I wanted to be when I grew up, I knew only one thing for sure. I told her, "I want to do nothing, just like you." (She still laughs her ass off about this.)

When she probed further I explained more clearly, "All I ever want to do, in my whole life, is to be a mommy." It was true. This was all I had ever wanted. I hated being an only child. I was determined to have a big family. Lots of kids, warmth, noise and chaos. I couldn't wait. I longed and ached, and couldn't wait to have them all... Myself.

It wasn't just parenthood I longed for, it was pregnancy itself. I couldn't wait to hold human life within me. I'd dreamt since my earliest memory about the miracle of childbirth, and the amazing gift that I, as a woman, would be able to experience it. For God's sake, according to my mother's story I was, personally, the first natural (unmedicated) birth in the entire University of Maryland teaching hospital. Whether she was factually correct or not, to me my own mother was a pioneer and I was proud of her. We'd talked about it a million times.

So, there I sat. 19-years-old. With Dr. Doctor and my mom, wringing her hands. And there I sat.

~

I have to tell you though, my friend, life is an interesting game. I was young, and I wasn't a huge fan of authority. I heard this doctor, and believe me I was traumatized, but I couldn't wrap my brain around the enormity of all of his words. So, I simply didn't. Somewhere in my lovely subconscious, I just chose not to. I accepted my fate, for the moment. I slept the right way, quit doing the sports I loved, and feared long car rides. I suppose the concept of marriage and family seemed far enough away that I was able to suspend that devastation, for a time.

I went back to Lehigh and completed my BA, moved to New York City, and lived my life. I experienced on and off chronic pain for years, but not another acute episode that rivaled the one during hell week. Life simply went on. When I held a baby, my back ached. When I waitressed, my back ached. When I had to stand or walk for a long time doing shit I didn't like to do, my back ached.

I noticed it. I lamented my fate as much as a person of my age and resilience could do. There was enough defiance in me, thankfully, to deny deny deny, and gently forget about it much of the time. This was largely because I was too busy being obsessed with my immediate needs; another beautiful affliction of youth. I steeped myself in this welcome pool of denial for quite a while. And, it worked. Trust me, I will never criticize you for your personal denial. Sometimes you really need it for the moment.

I did suffer, though. A lot. I was scared. I figured in the back of my mind that I probably wouldn't be a mom. If I was to be, it would likely be only one kid, the exact opposite of my master plan. The pain of such a fate was way too much to contemplate for the specific me. So basically, I didn't. That tree was falling in my little mind every day, though, *and I now know that I always felt in somewhere.*

One morning, miraculously, my mom was watching the Rosie O'Donnell show, when she had her original talk show. On that fateful episode, Rosie televised a plea that my mother reported as follows (hear a Jewish mother's voice, paraphrasing Rosie.) *Help my producer who is in a motorized wheelchair! She is in so much pain. It is ruining her life! Yet, no doctor or physical therapy has cured her!* Apparently, Rosie beseeched her viewers to write in if they had any ideas that might help. And they responded in droves.

They said, "Dr. John Sarno."[4]

My nearly hysterical mother called me (I was about 27 at this point) and said, "I know what's wrong with you!" I can't say enough about my love for my mother's certainty when she knows something. It's adorable.

71

"Rosie's producer used to be in a motorized wheelchair!" She is shrieking at this point. "And now she is doing *cartwheels* on stage!"

"Buy this book!" She begged: *Healing Back Pain* by Dr. John Sarno. And you bet your sweet ass, I did just that.

~♪

I read it. Well, I skimmed it. Well, I read the title page and the back cover. But anyway, whatever! I got it. Here is what I got, at the time:

> Regardless of what you have been told is wrong with you, when you are in pain you need to realize that you are also really, subconsciously angry. Actually, you are enraged. You don't know how angry you are, but your brain does. It is diverting your attention by physiologically enabling pain in your body. To relieve the pain, consider why you might be angry. Don't hide from it. Acknowledge it to yourself. There is no need to tell anyone else. Wait a little while (don't expect a miracle in the moment!) A little while later when you attend to your pain, it will be gone.

"That is lunatic," you might be thinking. I totally hear you. But here's the thing:

It worked.

As I was standing there waitressing the lunch shift, and although not a single person aside from staff was in the restaurant and we were not allowed to sit because it looked lazy, my back killed me. While I was standing in the kitchen doorway of the children's house in which I was nannying, hearing from their mother about the things I should be doing differently or better although she had no desire to actually participate in the raising of her own children, my back killed me. When I was spending time with a person who was selfish and unkind to me, and instead of speaking my mind I let them walk all over me, my back screamed.

So, I commenced an amazing and miraculous experiment, on myself. Instead of ruminating on my flawed anatomy, I decided to ponder, "Why am I so mad?"

Most of the time I got to it pretty quickly, somewhere in my young brain. Although only a small portion of Sarno's priceless information resonated at the time, and the real understanding that led me to my deeper truth came later, it was enough to cause a huge shift in me. I learned to give myself a moment's space and peace and say silently, in the privacy of my thoughts:

"I'm mad because I am standing here, and I am all messed up in my back. But I'm not gonna tell you that, Mr. Jerk-Off Restaurant Manager, or Mrs. Better-Than-Me-Who-Ignores-What's-Important-in-Life-But-Knows-Best, because maybe then you will think that I am *less than,* and you won't value me. Maybe you will discover that I'm not perfect. Perhaps you won't want to keep me on as an employee. I need the money. You have no idea how hard I am trying. You have no idea how hard my life is! I have to worry about all of this shit with my back, and money, and my parents, and my future... no one's life is harder than mine! I might not speak like this to anyone, but here I am standing in your stupid restaurant, or slaving in your overpriced house that you don't even appreciate, and no one is even *here,* and you aren't even doing anything! Plus, I resent doing this job in the first place, because I graduated with honors and I am awesome and I am smart and I have no idea what the hell I want to do with my life!"

I said that, or something like that, to myself. I was brave. I searched my brain for all of the uncensored reasons for which I could possibly be enraged. I screamed them silently, just to me. And I have to tell you straight up, it totally fucking worked. I would attend to the pain at some point later when the restaurant picked up with customers, or when I was involved in an activity with the kids, and I realized... I couldn't feel the pain. It was gone.

"Wow." "Weird." "Cool," I thought. Slowly, subconsciously, alongside these words and others in related situations, the fear began to seep away that I was a damaged product destined for compromise and pain. I disavowed the evil Dr. Doctor and decided tentatively, that everything might possibly be okay. And that actually worked.

For a while.

In fairness, it was a good long while. I completed the graduate work for my MSW, got married, carried two babies to term without back problems, or virtual death if you were listening to the drama of Dr. Doctor, and moved to the suburbs of New York City. I was living the dream. Right? Right?? I was certainly living the dream that I had laid out as a child, on paper. I'd promised myself openly by the age of 12 that I would create the family for myself that I hadn't been handed as a child. I was so determined. Way too determined, which I would eventually understand. Yet sadly, or thankfully depending on how you'd like to look at it, the story does not end here.

$\sim$

When my second baby Oliver was 10-months-old, he liked to walk around our backyard deck in a walker, as babies do before they can toddle. There were three short steps that led from the deck to the driveway, and I wanted to make sure he was safe. I didn't want him to walk his walker over the steps and land his soft little head on the asphalt.

I was being lazy. I didn't feel like taking the baby out and carrying his 20-pound-self and the large, awkward walker down separately. Not to mention, he couldn't stand yet and I didn't quite know where I would even put him during the transfer. Mostly though I was confident, or so I thought, that I was immune. It didn't occur to me that I might still be susceptible to the kind of pain that I had conquered. I simply didn't know, at the time, that I hadn't yet actually done the *real* work necessary to conquer it. I had been granted a taste of freedom. My sentence had been time served, and I had been released. I had no idea that the true test was yet to come. I didn't know that it was about more than reading the title page and the back cover.

I bent over and lifted the walker with him in it (all 20-pounds-of-baby and whatever that plastic thingie weighed,) and started down the three steps. By the second step, I felt it.

It was like a hot knife dragging, deeply and slowly, across my lower back. The pain was so dramatic that I can remember it, physically, all these years later. Miraculously, I found my footing enough to set the walker down gently onto the blacktop of the driveway. Then, in the shape of an L, I screamed to my friend that I was really hurt (like, really!) and stumbled into the house and onto the couch. It was a re-run of hell week 1991. Sadly though, "This time," I decided, "It was real."

The following weeks and months need not be described in detail. Just know this: more orthopedic surgeons, steroids, opiate pain meds, muscle relaxers, physical therapy 3x/week, electric stim treatments on the lower back, therapeutic massages (which only made me hurt more,) etc. To be honest with you, the worst part was that the pain had tricked me, completely. Regardless of all the knowledge I had acquired that I could be angry, rageful, terrified, and/or sad and still feel the physical pain instead of the emotion (my brain rescuing me) I was fully, full-on fooled.

I was, and am, human. Although I considered myself smart and savvy and informed, at that moment none of it mattered. I decided that I was sick and damaged, and so...I was. I cried myself to sleep, almost every night for a year. After I recovered from the initial acute incident and settled into the lovely life of chronic pain, I lamented the new truth that I would never parent actively, as I had dreamed. I was impatient with my kids. When I bent over to change a diaper and they were being fussy, I yelled at them. I needed people to help me lift them into cribs and cars. I stopped going to places that might tax me too much. I hated my fate. I hated everything and everybody and everything.

But I didn't ponder that hatred, or anything I had learned in my 20's. Instead I obsessed, constantly, about my broken body and my broken life.

My personal surrender came during a moment to which most parents can relate. I was in a deli where all the lovely candies and crunchy treats were displayed in clear containers, at the eye level and hand level of three-foot-tall people. I was attempting to pay at the counter. My daughter Isabella aged 3, began to loudly and joyfully grab containers of licorice and gummy worms. I pried each out of her little hands, only to have her grab another. Oliver, who was almost 2, caught wind that this was delightful. He joined in emphatically.

Each of them was now wildly double-fisting Swedish fish and yogurt covered pretzels, threatening to unknowingly dump the contents everywhere as the lids were being rocked. I was trying to pay and pry in tandem desperately, choking back tears of embarrassment and... um.... what else? I had no clue. All I remember thinking was, "Get me the hell out of here. Now."

I finally managed to pay and leave the deli. I had one hand gripping the 3-year-old's, and the other locked on the wrist of the toddler. As we traversed the parking lot, I felt the pain building. I felt my back stiffening. I felt my fear, well I thought I felt it. Now I know I felt it, big time. We arrived at the minivan. And here is the horrible truth of that moment: I locked up in pain and I couldn't do anything. I was frozen in agony.

I couldn't get the car keys out of my bag without letting go of one of them, in an active parking lot. I couldn't open the door of the car. I couldn't reach my phone. Even if I could have managed that far, I couldn't imagine lifting either of them into a car seat and buckling it properly. I couldn't even shift the way in which I was holding their perpetually wriggling limbs. I couldn't do anything.

And there was no one to help me. I was alone.

I did the only thing I could do. I held onto them as hard as I could. I stood there in that parking lot. I rested my forehead on the driver's side window of my car, and I cried. I sobbed. I sobbed for my sorry self, and my poor children who had to endure my failure. I sobbed in embarrassment and self-pity. I cried for the fact that I was fucking everything up. I wept for how pathetic I looked. I held their wrists, and I cried. I was as desperate as I have ever been. After a while they gave up the fight, the way kids do sometimes, when they get in some unknown way that there is nothing to be done. They just stood there with me. I don't remember how long we stood there.

Eventually, I got myself together. Minutes? Hours? To this day, I have no idea. But somehow I was able to get them into the car. Probably for all the rage and sadness that head been unleashed in my surrender. I drove home and got them into bed, and sat down on my own bed. I stared into the black night through the window of my bedroom, and somewhere in that moment of desperation, I said to myself, "I don't know if the doctors are right with all of their diagnoses and explanations of how my back is falling apart, or Dr. Sarno is a miracle worker with all his power of the mind rhetoric. But I don't care. Mess with me, but don't mess with my kids."

I was ready to do anything.

Dr. Sarno, the widely published author with a cult-like following of celebrities and news personalities, was expensive. [5] My mom paid. She had next to nothing, but she paid because at the time I couldn't. That meant a lot. I wasn't going to mess around with this chance I was getting.

He examined me, as many medical professionals had done over the years. He looked at my X-Rays and my MRIs. He categorically dismissed the *novel* I had written in preparation for the appointment detailing every moment I had encountered back pain, and what I had done about it. He told me to stop bending at the knees, instead of the waist. He told me that my films didn't lie, but every human's body becomes flawed as he or she grows and changes and gets bumped around. He said that although I looked damaged inside, this "damage" did not account for my pain. He told me what I needed to do. It sounded hard to believe. It felt so scary, as it occurred to me how terrified I would be if it didn't work. It sounded too simple to be true.

But, it didn't matter to me how it sounded. I was desperate to be better. I had surrendered, and I was open to any possibility the universe might hand me. I was sick and tired of being sick and tired. I would do anything.

# CHAPTER 7

## *JournalSpeak*

"This above all; to thine own self be true."
WILLIAM SHAKESPEARE

**H**ere is what I did, what the good doctor told me I needed to do:

I needed to take a long, hard look at my life. Not the usual look that *Webster's Dictionary* defines, and not just my life today. This lovely look entailed shamelessly contemplating, in addition to the exhausting combo which I called my daily existence, my childhood, my ageless patterns, and my very personality which caused me to yearn always to be right and good. The reason *Webster's* failed me was that this kind of looking was not based on the word's definition I had understood at the time. Instead, in some intangible way my intuition told me that this process would involve more insight than had ever been required in my life.

This internal investigation was (and is) not something that can be done haphazardly, during random spurts of time which we like to call free. I was instructed to assign blocks of time, each day, that were purely for me. And I had to *journal*.

First up, I was told to make three lists under the headings: **Childhood, Daily Life, Personality**. The *childhood* list should be comprised of my brain's outermost reachings of every event or relationship in my childhood from which I remembered sadness or pain, conflict, or trauma. In plain english, I had to transcribe my tapes of growing up in a bulleted list. I didn't realize at the time (but I certainly know now) that the stories which inspired the items on my list weren't necessarily the healing truths I needed, yet they were imperative to begin the bunny trail that would lead me there. Sometimes I explain it like this to clients: Think of your conscious issues on the lists each as the end of a pirate's treasure map - the "X marks the spot." Once each location is revealed, it's time to do the most important task. Wanna guess what it is? C'mon... give it a try!

Ding Ding Ding! That's right, folks. Then, you have to dig.

The same was true of the list for *daily life*. This list was to comprise of day-to-day dealings which stressed me enough to take note, whether they involved work, family responsibilities, friendships, my annoying neighbor, etc. There were no hard, fast rules except one: be thorough, and never dismiss anything for appearing unimportant.

The last list, *personality*, was a little harder to envision. The items on this list needed to embody the essence of me, created by my nature and my childhood experiences, which I held onto like a baby blanket. Things like, "I need to be well-liked by everyone or I feel uncomfortable and inadequate," or, "I feel the need to please everyone all the time, even if I am the only one left hurting." The biggest and hardest one for me personally was, "I need to be perfect. If I can't be perfect, I may as well not be at all."

The goal was to examine each item on my lists until the pain began to subside, and then even longer. I was to journal it out as long as it took to leave the pain behind completely. Sounds like hippie dippie hocus pocus pie in the sky insanity, right? Well, maybe so. The question is: *How long would you like to suffer?* Because every single person I know to have tried this with an earnest open mind, has gotten better. Your call.

So, here we are. We have arrived at the heart of the matter, the way in which this kind of journaling can end your pain and transform your life. I am willing to share this deeply personal experience with you because I know that simple instructions don't always do it justice. You need to feel it - not only how difficult it was for me to admit this stuff to myself - but how long I had kept it pushed far down in my psyche.

I am about to give you a gift that almost no one gives one another person. I am going to share with you my raw humanity, regardless of how it might hurt me to tell you, or how it might affect my loved ones who could potentially misinterpret it. So please, just listen and hear. Respect me enough to give yourself this chance to understand. I am imparting to you a unique insight. Cherish it. Perhaps it will entice you to cherish yourself.

~⁏

The journaling I did with the help of Dr. Sarno's theories represents the biggest epiphany of my life. The act of deciding to do something different in order to heal myself transcended from simple pain relief into the informing of my entire life, and in turn my therapeutic practice and the writing of this book.

I discovered something so transformative, that the moment I uncovered it I immediately understood it to be both Godly and un-Godly at the same time. It was, all at once, ugly and repulsive and intensely beautiful. I saw the reason that we are all so full of shit without even knowing it, and injuring ourselves so constantly in the process. I understood why we all suffer. I found the tool I needed (we all need) to stop all of our destructive certainty. *I found the language that heals.*

I forged a path for myself that served to free me from much of my physical, as well as emotional pain. In doing so, I came to understand that the traditional definitions of many words I had spoken for years had been trapping me in a jail out of which, I held the key. I suffered in the birth of it, as I did with my children and as any person suffers as he or she moves from deep darkness into light. I coined this language of truth *JournalSpeak.*

Here is how it went down.

~⁏

So, I'm sitting in the dirty deli (only about 6 people will get this reference) with my legal pad and a sharpened pencil. I am determined. I will unleash the demons of my mind! I will whine and complain about my screwed-up childhood, the failings of my parents, the stress of my daily life that leads me to stay up all night with insomnia, the frustrations of parenthood! My crap, down on paper. Ok, Dr. Sarno. Here you go.

I write a little blah blah blah about my upbringing, and my overly critical father. I transcribe my tapes for a while. I recount a few stories which I have been telling for years, about stuff that went down when I was 10, or 12, or... I don't even know.

It feels fine, I guess. If I am to be honest with myself at the moment, it probably feels like a whole lot of nothing. Yet, I am being a good student, naturally. I am following directions. I am doing as I have been taught to do.

Feeling bored, I move onto the *daily life* column. I choose: Motherhood. Please note that this moment is only a week or two after the horror of the parking lot incident described earlier. So, recall that my oldest daughter is 3, and my son, almost 2.

I scrawl motherhood at the top of my page, and I start to write. I no longer have the hard copy, in fact I threw it in the trash that day. Yet I remember, painfully (forgive the pun) well.

"I am so tired. The baby is up a lot, and my daughter is really a baby herself, still. Less than 22 months apart! This wasn't the plan. It is so hard for me. My husband is always busy. Working working working. He has an important job, so I just have to deal. But I feel so alone in all of this."

And then, something happened in me; to me. Something happened that is likely the most significant shift in thinking that I have ever experienced: I felt uneasy, like I was lying.

I wasn't actually lying, of course. The feelings on the page were true to me. But, something was missing. I felt an enormous sense of guilt, coupled with a debt of gratitude. My mom had spent over a thousand dollars so I could see this Dr. Miracle for half an hour. I needed to honor that! I wanted to. I realized, somewhere in there, that this was not the journaling that was going to save me. I needed to be braver. More real. More true. I had no clue where this was going at the time, but somewhere deep down, I got it. I got something.

And I wrote:

No. No, that's not it. Not really what I need to know. These can't possibly be the reasons that my body is wracked with pain. What is it?? What isssssss ittttttttttttttt??? Why do you suffer, Nicole????? TELL ME!!!!!!!!! FUCKING TELL ME!!!!!!!!! Stop being polite. You are a fucking coward. Stop it. Do this! DO THIS THE WAY YOU ARE SUPPOSED TO! You wanna be such a fucking good girl???? Then, BE ONE!

I wrote, on that fateful day, in my sweet little dirty deli, on my yellow-lined-legal-pad, something that has saved the lives of a few people. These people are myself, and my three incredible kids. And, if you can bring yourself to believe in or simply conceive of my religion of human connectedness and loving kindness, maybe it will save your life too.

Here is truth, my friend. The first raw personal truth I ever knew, the first line of *JournalSpeak* ever penned. I wouldn't have had the need to even consider it much less seek it, had I not been so desperate.

But I was, and I was ripe with surrender, and here is what came forth. Understand that your *JournalSpeak* truth might shock you initially, as it is necessary to redefine the way people are permitted to think. Also understand, that this is the only key on the ring that will open your jail cell. Do you think that you might be tired of sitting in there? Ok kid, here you go. From me, to you. Always fresh, never frozen. I wrote:

~

"It is not that I am tired. It is not that everything is too much.

It's that I hate being a mother.

I hate everything about this life, and I think my kids can feel it, especially my daughter. She doesn't love me, I can tell. When she cries it's not to me, it's at me. She smiles at other people more than she smiles at me. She has curly blond hair. I have long, straight hair that is so brown it looks black. She was "supposed" to look like me, but she doesn't. Everyone says she looks just like my husband.

And he isn't even around enough to have a clue about her.

I pour everything I have into being a mother and my kids don't even care. They hate me. Plus, I don't even know how to love two children! My mom taught me everything, but she only had one. I have no roadmap. I feel alone all of the time. I feel fat and inadequate. I feel like my best days are behind me and I'm only 32.

I thought I knew exactly what I wanted, and I knew nothing. I've done everything wrong and now I have babies and I can never take that back and I am ruined. I have the wrong life, and I am trapped in it forever."

~

Sounds harsh, huh? Unthinkable, even. Flies in the face of every tip you learned while reading *What to Expect: The First Year*.

Yeah, I hear you.

Here is the miracle, though, my human friend. Here is what this diatribe turned into, pretty much immediately.

"Stop! Wait."

"That doesn't feel true either! I don't hate my kids and my life. This is crazy. If I sit with that for one second it feels like as big a lie as anything. What the hell is it, then?! Where is all this anger directed?? WHY DOES IT FEEL LIKE I HATE EVERYTHING I'VE EVER WANTED?? WHO THE HELL AM I? WHAT AM I FEELING???"

This bravery set me free, and all of a sudden I knew. And I've never looked back.

"I know! I KNOW. I am mad at MYSELF. I am ENRAGED. Whom do I hate? WHOM DO YOU HATE, NICOLE?"

I hated myself.

"I hate myself for my stupidity and naiveté. For all of those years when I lived for this rigid, fucking fantasy of what motherhood would be. I took it for granted - having a baby and being a mom was going to be perfect, amazing, rewarding, great! I would be mother earth, and my kids would feel the strength of my love and immediately adore me! There would be nothing but bliss. Sure I would be tired, but I wouldn't care in the light of my joy. Pregnancy would be a miracle, and I would revel in it... not feel fat, used-up, zitty, and sick all the time."

What a fool I was. What a sweet, hopeful, lovely fool I was. Just like you in your own stories, once you are bold enough to take a true look at them. It's the same for that girl across the room from you, and the man who just served you coffee, and the kid who fixed your computer the other day.

How amazing the blindness, of such a lovely fool. How amazing the power.

I view myself as this smart evolved person, and I had literally no idea that all of this thinking was going on in my unconscious brain. None. Yet now I know - it was, constantly. That tree was falling in my mental forest every day. And since those dark, hateful thoughts were impossible for my sweet polite kind self to even conceive, I shut them out. I pushed them down, way down. I soothed myself with societal truths: all new mothers are tried, scared, confused, worried and overwhelmed. This may be true, but it wasn't what was keeping me in pain. What was keeping me in pain was, that in the most primitive inconceivable unthinkable way, I fucking hated my life as a result. That is, until my whole world cracked wide open, and I understood that it wasn't the babies and motherhood I hated. It was me.

Yet, before you gasp in judgment, you must hear the last, most beautiful, amazing healing part - the prize at the end of the scavenger hunt! The same reason that any of this dredged-up sewage means anything other than pain.

The moment I allowed this unthinkable truth into my conscious mind, the moment I stopped fighting subconsciously so hard not to feel this intangible ugliness and just allowed my deeper truth to rise within me...

I was free.

My mind opened up so big, and I saw my whole life - my expectations and my misconceptions, my dreams based on fear. My sad little self who just wanted (needed, desperately) to finally have a big connected family, with me as the matriarch. My need to be loved for Who I Am instead of Who I Can Be for You.

It hit my like a tsunami of truth. The power of that moment still affects me, today. I wrote:

"I am a mother. My God. I'm humbled with gratitude. I love both of my babies, for whom... for everything that they are. I don't need to be disappointed and enraged! I don't need to live within those little girl notions which have served only to blind me from the joy which is right here before me.

In fact, this isn't even vaguely about my kids; it is all about me. And if it's about me, I have the power to recognize it and then, to change it.

I'm not angry at anyone but me, and now that I see my truth, I can work on not being so angry anymore. My discontent is only an illusion that my inner dialogue has created! I can now work on healing the issues around my parents, and my upbringing. My pain was born there, as it was there that the seeds of my expectations were sown.

Yet, I'm just a human person - a product of the experiences which have shaped me, and more importantly, the person I have created as a result.

It's ok. It can really be ok.

I need to forgive myself now. There is nothing to be gained by suffering forever in self-hatred and self-doubt. I can't allow myself to do this, even if it feels bizarrely easier. I have a job to do. I need to raise these kids. I want to teach them to love themselves. If they can do this, and throughout their lives learn who they are and what they think about things, then they will have the most important tools in life!"

Rich with these realizations, I was opened. I was opened up to love so much more. It was no longer necessary to dance as fast as I could to stop feeling the disappointments of my life. This sadness was only a ruse, a perception born from old stories which were no longer serving me. I didn't need protection from my feelings - I needed to feel them! And it turned out those feelings were of joy and gratitude and love, once those protective mechanisms which were poisoning me were removed.

Within a couple days, my back pain diminished by about 80%. I'm not kidding.

I don't want to make this whole story about physical pain. What began for me as a journey into solving a physical issue, morphed quickly into a personal philosophy which applied to all pain: physical, emotional, spiritual and mental. It also applies to the countless human struggles in our lives: being trapped in our patterns, slaves to our self-inflicted judgments, mired in our resentments, locked within our certainties regarding *who we think we are.*

~

Having said all of this heavy stuff, I don't want to leave you hanging so I will finish this long tale.

Soon after this revelation and others related to my formerly unconscious disappointment, anger, fear, sadness etc., I was able to find many places of deeper truth within myself. As we've discussed, truth exists on two levels. The surface level is certainly valid, and in no way are we liars when we play these tapes. Yet, the deeper level of one's true truth is what heals.

This particular story which I am sharing with you began in April, 2005. Today, as I sit in this breezy cafe on the beach writing to you, it is April, 2016. I have been largely pain-free since. On some days, depending on the conflicts in my life, I have experienced various pains and afflictions. Yet, in the midst of such I have never again been scared. I have never thrown myself into a panic regarding, "What is wrong with me?" or "What should I do?" I simply turn my thoughts and my journal toward my truth. I search curiously and openly for the roots of my pain, anger and frustration. I open myself to that which entraps me - that which feels insurmountable. I'm not scared to acknowledge new feelings as they present themselves to me. Within this raw bravery I am saved, again and again. If you think this sounds impossible, I can only tell you that it's true. Not just for me, but for countless others with whom I've had the pleasure to share this journey. It's the greatest blessing of my life.

Deeper truth needs to be blatantly unmasked in order for you to know what is really meaningful to you, and what you might be hiding behind in order not to feel. Do you think that I hate being a mother?

I say to you, with the loveliest teary-eyed smile, No. Being a mother is the single greatest joy and accomplishment of my life. I say this not because if I did hate motherhood it would be an impossible issue to overcome with personal work, or even because I am intent on protecting my kids from this knowledge. I say this because I was actually correct when I was ten. I am meant to be a mom - I'm really fantastic at it. Here's the thing, though. I wouldn't have been. I would have been self-involved and judgmental, angry critical and controlling. I would have tried to shape them based on my issues and the old stories which whispered constantly into my ears. I would've been like my dad.

I also say this because my oldest daughter is 13, and she made me a parent. She is completing the 8th grade. She is delightfully sassy, and thoughtfully wise. She says things I could never anticipate, regardless of my worldly prowess. Her sense of humor ignites me with joy, again and again. She causes me to redefine my book-smarted view of parenting. She has unique ideas that will clearly have great power. She is a person in the world whose essence has nothing, yet everything to do with me. Witty and smart, edgy, funny and outlandish. She is so like me in so many ways, and so unlike me in others, most of which I admire. She is boldly confident, helplessly in need of attention, and hopelessly dramatic. She is in love with love (which kills me because I wish to save her,) yet she is safe because I know my truth, and I won't try to do so. She knows who she is, which I never did at her age.

Our children have room to be who they are when our own disappointments and resentments are ours, not theirs. The child I just described is a child raised by a parent who has taken the time to understand her own truth. I respect my children's ideas. I respect their opinions. I can't wait to see what they become. I miss them when they are away from me. I love that they admire me. I parent and discipline them. And, most of the time when I can control myself, our struggles are about them, not about me playing out my damage on their sweet little self-esteems. That feels good; *that* feels true. I never feel like a liar anymore.

It has taken some serious insight, but my truth has included:

My kids are a pain in the ass, but they are also my best friends and my greatest cheering squad. They respond beautifully to my love and acceptance, and when I watch them adjust their behavior simply to please me, the primitive little girl in me jumps for joy. Then, I forgive myself for that.

They take me for granted. They tell me what they think, without fear of anger or retribution. They cry when they are mad at themselves, although they protest to be mad at each other. When they are ready they tell me all about it, and we understand together what really went on.

I am grateful every day that I figured out how to do this whole crazy thing called parenting without making it all about me. Don't think for one minute I am pulling the high and mighty card. Those ungrateful monsters drive me crazy too! I lose my patience. I lose my temper. Sometimes I completely lose my shit. It just doesn't last longer than it needs to.

It can't, when it's not about you. I can't tell you how important it is for every parent to think about this one sentence.

I thank every God (who or which) exists for my debilitating pain because as a result, strange as it seems, I am doing right by my kids, and myself. I absolutely wouldn't be, if I was still mired in my own bullshit.

My personal (ugly stupid real honest insane hidden beautiful misunderstood) crap, which I learned to gently allow in without fear in order to come to my truth, saved my ability to parent. It saved my ability to enjoy anything in my life. I had never really hated being a mother, and although I had subconsciously hated myself, in the end that didn't really matter anymore. The self-hatred dissipated into the air the moment of my confession; it lost its power completely. The only thing that mattered was: My truth set me free.

It revealed me, and then it allowed me the space to forgive myself. It relieved my pain, and introduced me to the parent and person I really wanted and needed to be. In this beauty, I became what we all needed - the kids and me. Herein, we arrive at the most important lesson of this chapter, and this whole book:

None of this would've come to pass had it not been for my discovery and recognition of the importance of *JournalSpeak*.

I had to just *say it*, regardless of the ugliness. So do you. I needed to do this, and I had to write it down even if I just turned around and ripped it to sheds into a public garbage can. I had to do this for myself, without the fear of judgment, and without my self-imposed scrutiny which seemed to accompany me everywhere.

Each of our truths is layered and complicated, and the bravery to attempt *JournalSpeak* is the first step to understanding the mystery that keeps us stuck. That which we privately think, openly speak, or even haltingly write does not define us. There is nothing which defines us, save our actions born of genuine intention. If you can release your

polite, full-of-crap self for just a second, you can show me that you understand. Show yourself. If you can, you'll have a chance to leave all the
trappings of misery behind. Give it a try.

Try it! Why not? No one is looking. I'm not even looking! I'm
lying on my couch, exhausted from my 5 million kids. I'm telling you,
my human friend, life can be better.

Let's go.

# CHAPTER 8

# Examples

"Alone we can do so little; together we can do so much."
HELEN KELLER

Y ou think you might wanna do this? Maybe, yes. Maybe you're a scared little fluffy puppy. I get it, either way. I want to try and make life easier. Here's the deal.

Every person who sits across from me in my office will soon hear my speech on the family that is my practice. "We are all in it together," I tell each newbie. "Each one of you who sits there, me, my family, our friends - we all suffer in the same ways, and we all heal in the same ways."

I will, in the course of our therapy when I see that you need it, share someone else's story. Sometimes it will be my story. Either way, it will allow you to lift your thoughts away from your own life, and into a space where understanding is more likely. You will never be able to identify anyone personally and no one could ever know your story was yours - I always make sure of that. Just know that sharing our humanity allows us to learn and grow from one another. Every day, I learn from you. We are all a family, and together we can do more than any of us could ever do alone. We help each other along.

Having said this, I would like to share some stories with you today. When you see us all, perhaps you will cultivate the bravery to more fully see yourself. Equally important is that these examples will serve to il-lustrate the translation from surface truth to *JournalSpeak*. My hope is that you will begin to envision a roadmap to guide you on this journey.

A peek into someone else's humanity can have great power. Names, ages, sexual preferences, religions, genders, hairstyles, etc. have been changed to protect the (quasi) innocent. When we're talking about me, I'll just full-on let you know. Here we go: Examples.

Example Number One: Mikey

Mikey grew up in a large Irish Catholic family, and was the baby of the group. The major baby; he was 12 years younger than his next sibling. He was the mistake. Mikey had genuinely come to terms with this fact, and spoke about it freely. I believed him.

When he entered therapy, Mikey told me that he was feeling unsuccessful at his job as a Middle School Administrator. He was widely respected as far as he could tell, and all of his annual reviews were generally positive. Yet both at work and in his personal life, Mikey insisted on constantly apologizing for seemingly insignificant failings. This practice of self-deprecation became so apparent that I needed to instruct him regularly during our sessions to stop worrying about me or what I thought, and to quit prefacing every story wildly in order to not offend me. I told him I was unoffendable. Eventually, he believed me.

Mikey's biggest presenting issue however, and we agreed upon this, was his inability to leave (or find happiness within) his reportedly abusive marriage. His wife Donna's behavior toward him was extremely demoralizing and passive-aggressively shaming. She would regularly smile in social situations as she painfully insulted him as he stood right beside her claiming, "It was just a *joke*. You're way too sensitive!"

She would pit his young daughters against him, going as far as telling them that Mikey didn't have time for them and was abandoning the family when he had to go away for a long weekend to care for his mother after a hip replacement. To be fair, I can't speak without bias in terms of this woman, because I have never met her. She had been invited countless times to join our sessions, yet consistently declined, stating:

"Therapy is for weak people," (Mikey's words as an expression of Donna's feelings.) "I don't need crutches to live my life. If you must do it, fine. Obviously it means that you are the one causing all the problems! What choice do I have other than endure your crap?"

To each her own, I always say. In terms of Mikey, I can tell you one thing I knew for sure. My client was suffering. He knew it, and he wanted out even if this meant confronting many painful realities involving children, money and family. He understood that he was living the most damaging kind of lie: The lie one knows about. I watched it killing him, slowly.

His daily life was challenging as it was wrought with bouts of anxiety, and sometimes panic attacks. He had back and neck pain that was often debilitating enough to keep him out of work for days. Sometimes he took more than the recommended dose of his prescribed painkillers, and we both worried that he might be on the brink of addiction. At night, he would dream of situations in which he was being arrested or chased leaving him paranoid, exhausted and unsettled.

Mikey was not still married to Donna for love, or companionship, or societal pressure (half of his friends were divorced) or even for their kids whom he truly believed would be better off if they split. The tension and arguing in their home couldn't be healthy for them. He couldn't find the words to tell me why he was with her. He was dying to know. He had schemed secretly to leave her several times, but he hit emotional wall after wall right before he was to carry out his plan. He often spoke of not wanting to be alone. Yet when he was pressed, Mikey could not seem to reconcile this specific feeling with being apart from Donna. "Why?" He used to ask me, almost begging, "Why? Why do I not have the strength to leave her? What is *wrong* with me?"

The answer was clear to me, personally: Fear. (Canned applause.)

You might be saying, "Thank you, Captain Obvious." I know. Fine, don't give me the genius grant yet. Stay with me. We have yet to answer the question, *Fear of what?*

Here is an imperative point - a really important truth about truth. The truths we uncover cannot wield the power of real, helpful freeing truths unless we can connect them to why we are struggling…today.

Let's repeat this another way: Old patterns live within us. We follow their rules like second nature. We go through their motions without much thought, until we are tapped on the shoulder. This tap can take the form of many things we've discussed. Perhaps it's an awakening to conscious misery in a relationship, "I just can't do this anymore!" It could manifest as physical pain (read: my back) or any issue or condition which goads us enough to feel it too strong to ignore. Once we are tapped, or poked, or bullied enough times by our unfelt emotion, we are usually handed a bag of shit labeled, "chronic pain" or "inexplicable exhaustion" "constant conflict" "painful indecision" "emotional paralysis" "despair" "depression" "panic attacks" "eating disorder" etc. We then strap ourselves into the lovely roller coaster described earlier: Pain and suffering, to Desperation, to Surrender, to… (finally) Openness to truth.

Your ancient self-destructive patterns through your brave work as a warrior of truth, can be unmasked, revealed and then applied to your struggles today. This often begins with defining one's particular, current brand of pain or fear or sad or *stuck*, and then connecting this present day reality with the place from which it grew, long ago. Once this massively important life-saving connection is established, we have bridged the perilous gap between your deeper truth and your current behavior. Now listen carefully. I'm only going to say this a hundred times.

Once you discover why you are doing something self-destructive, and once you can see that the patterns you are playing out no longer apply to your current life and are no longer serving you… you don't need to repeat them anymore! Hand on key, key in lock of jail, lock turning in door, door flung open. And, finally, you are free.

~෧

I am going to pretend that we are in the speed round at the end of a game show. I am going to attempt to illustrate for you the meaning of the above rant, as played out in Mikey's life.

Important: In order to open your mind to best allow this in, you need to embrace the following givens:

a)  I know a lot about the guy at this point in time, so my insights are based on deep, real knowledge.
b)  Nothing ever really goes this fast, or can be this simplified.
c)  Each person's journey is a process that cannot be rushed. Expecting pitfalls and occasional mental quicksand will protect you from game-ending defensiveness.

If you look at these conversations, as we are going to do right now, through the lens of time lapse photography they can be very beautiful. For you, this exercise can be transformative in understanding how the concept of *JournalSpeak* can allow each person to evolve toward deeper truth. You will see how it is possible to find freedom from all of your subconsciously self-imposed barriers. The moment in which I witness people connect with their misunderstood, primitive truths has such raw power. Once these truths are linked to current struggles, humans gain so much peace and perspective that any necessary changes flow naturally through their lives. I have the astounding privilege to see this, nearly every day. What an amazing gift! It humbles me. Having said all this.

I give you:  *Mikey, in session.*

Me:        What is upsetting you the most?

Him:       That I can't seem to find the strength to leave Donna.

Me:        Try to calm your mind, and tell me from your quietest, most honest place: What is the most torturous thought related to leaving her?

Here he takes a long moment for thought, which is followed by this very deep truth for Mikey - one he has never shared with me, or anyone (or himself, as I later discovered) before:

Him:       The image of her sleeping with other men. I can hardly believe it, but it feels the most true. Even as I say it, it sounds foolish. Because I don't even want her!

Me:        Ok, let's look at that. You don't want her to be with other men, even once you split. Why do you think?

Him:       The most powerful feeling I can come up with is that I would hate for them to be better in bed than me... that they could satisfy her in a way I couldn't, or didn't.

Me:        Good insight. Let's take it further. What is so bad about another man satisfying her, when you don't want her yourself?

Him:       Because he would be better. I wouldn't be best... I don't know.... (he trails off, a bit lost.)

Here is where I get to be the badass therapist. It is the moment when I get to utilize the months of stories and tears and insight which this generous person has shared with me, and connect the dots to really help him.

Me:        I think I know.

Him:       Please! Rescue me! (We kid like that.)

Me:        Remember when we talked about your childhood, and being the baby "by far," and having to sit at home alone with babysitters while your parents busied themselves with all of the older kids? And once they got around to paying attention, they were too tired or impatient to deal with you? And how you ached for your father's attention? So much, and so painfully?

Him:     (emotional, raw) Yes.

Me:      You told me. The only time he looked your way was when you were the best athlete for the moment, or you had the hottest girlfriend. And as you grew and became more desperate to get his respect and attention, you would even make up fake awards and convince him that you had won First Place? And it worked. Remember, you were so ashamed to tell me?

Him:     It's hard even to think about it now. I was so sad. I wanted him so much. And he didn't want me. Unless...

Me:      (gently) Right... And so you were. You created a boy who was the *best*, and for a moment he saw you.

Him:     (Quite emotional) I'm still doing that with him, you know.

Me:      I know.


Me:      Mikey, I'm starting to think that the panic that seems to grip you each time you make a move to leave Donna is strongly connected to this. You know why? Because what did it feel like in your world, if you were't the best?

Him:     If I really think about it, when my father wasn't looking at me, I felt invisible. When I wasn't the best, I wasn't even in the room.

Me:      Right. And these feelings don't rest until we uncover them for what they are today. As a little boy, if you weren't the best you weren't seen at all... You didn't feel as if you were a person worthy of love and attention.

Him:     I felt worthless and alone.

Here's what happened, so we can skip to the last page of this proverbial book. Mikey and I, from a simple truth which seemed insignificant to him until it rose in our session, were able to connect his ancient - but still very real panic - over not being perceived as the *man satisfying Donna* directly with his inability to leave her. As you might imagine, the fears generated from this deep place were attached to far more than just sex. They were pervasive, and touched upon everything in his life from what other people would think of him as a father, to how their couple friends would talk about him, to his potential inability to be effective at work because people would see him as pathetic. Put together, all these whirling thoughts served to paralyze him, as they created so many spaces in which being the best was not possible. Why?

Because until he really looked carefully at the truth as it lived within him, he still felt the same unconscious feelings as did his 7-year-old self: If I leave Donna, I am not the best, and if I'm not the best, I am invisible. I don't even exist. You may think this stuff sounds silly, but it literally kept a man standing still for ten years of his life. Ten years.

As soon as Mikey was able to identify the "black hole of emptiness in his chest" as he called it, he was able to recognize that he wasn't really that scared to leave Donna. He was actually decently calm about the process. He just hadn't understood how the power of his feelings of worthlessness and judgement left over from childhood were masquerading as panic around being alone. In reality he was just still a little boy looking out the window, waiting for his parents to come home with his brothers and sisters, feeling alone and sad and impossible to love.

And invisible.

Almost comically, we discovered together, Mikey was really looking forward to being alone, and not having to endure the pain of a relationship which he had tried unsuccessfully for years, to improve. Not long after the final session in this synopsis, Mikey, with peace and confidence, ended his unhealthy marriage. In the following months through work related to these epiphanies, his back and neck pain waned, and soon vanished completely. He stopped taking prescription painkillers before he became physically addicted. I still see him, and we still excavate his truth as he navigates these new waters, but the mystery which surrounded a 10 year struggle is now solved.

And so it goes.

~

Example Number Two: *The Movie I Saw Last Week*

This may seem a somewhat odd second example for an accomplished therapist who's had so many profound tales of healing in her practice. To be honest with you, I had no plans of writing about this. That is, until last night. When the realization hit me however, it felt too significant to ignore. Read the next example, and you be the judge of its power. I am always open to dissent.

Last week after the kids were asleep, Tiff and I decided to find a grown-up movie to watch as so often we must endure the horror of tweeny-bopper sit coms. As we scrolled through the On Demand menu which has become the definition of America's discontent with the 40,000 channels on TV, we came upon a David Cronenberg film entitled, *A Dangerous Method.* In a nutshell, it is the somewhat fictionalized true story about the bizarre yet brilliant relationship between Sigmund Freud and Carl Jung in the early 1900's, and the birth of Psychoanalysis as a result.

So, we are watching this film and Keira Knightley (brilliantly, I think) plays a woman named Sabina Spielrein who is so insane that the viewer has no choice but to become physically uncomfortable while watching her. She fights and curses and contorts her body in such a violent fashion, it is hard to believe that she could ever even hold a coherent conversation. Naturally, this behavior unfolds as she is being actively institutionalized, and her doctor is, (lucky girl)... Carl Jung!

As she thrashes around like a maniac and tells her attendants to screw-off as she defiantly swims, fully-clothed, in a pond on the premises, Jung remains unfazed. He speaks to her like a human being. He takes walks with her on the grounds of the hospital without fear. He decides to test his new theory of "the talking method" on her.

We soon learn that he and Freud in tandem, although separately in separate cities, have a similar revolutionary theory that *talking about ones problems can solve major personal issues without any other interventions*. In attempting this therapy with Sabina he insists that she sit in front of him, so she cannot meet his gaze - anyone familiar with Analysis will understand this. If you are unfamiliar with this form of treatment, I will explain. Psychoanalysts advise patients to either lay on a couch, or sit in some fashion where they do not need to regard the therapist. The idea is that the patient will be less blocked in revealing that which arises in the mind if he or she can "free associate," an exercise of opening one's mind without restrictions, and this process is hampered if he or she has to face the therapist. In turn, the hope is that the patient will look within, instead of without. Although this is not my strictly chosen method, I can understand and strongly respect the concept.

In any case, the viewer is brought to understand that Sabina comes from a respectable family and has been highly educated. Jung sits her down to talk, and in brutal sessions which are rough to watch, we learn that she has been horribly abused by her father. At first, one is (at least I was) traumatized by hearing what this poor woman has had to endure: Vicious beatings, as young as 4-years-old, *naked*, for spilling her milk.

You sit there watching this horror, and you say to yourself, "No wonder she is insane."

Yeah, but wait.

In their last session we witness at the Institution, Jung is inquiring more deeply about the beatings, and he asks Sabina, "How did you feel when your father ordered you to go into the little room, naked, to be beaten?"

Stuttering and gagging and choking on her own admission she screams, "Excited!"

So now you stop in your tracks, and you're like, "Huh? Did I just hear that correctly?" Yes. Yes, you did.

Herein, we arrive at: The Example of: Sabina Spielrein.

The scene goes on to reveal an incredibly truthful, painful, disgusting, shameful, heart-wrenching, disturbing, healing conversation in which Sabina admits with palpable panic and horror that the beatings caused her to be incredibly sexually aroused. I mean, this stuff is seriously dark. This woman is so tortured by what she is revealing that she almost vomits. She convulses and wretches as she tells Jung that she gets so excited by the concept of being beaten, that even the notion of it compels her to hide and masterbate almost immediately; obsessively.

The scene ends with Sabina's staunch - yet somewhat calmer - declaration that she is vile and disgusting, and should be locked-up in the Institution for life. The (non-Nicole) viewer is left trembling in the wake of her shocking truth; her destroyed humanity. I (Nicole) was left, mouth agape in shock, but for a completely different reason: I knew *exactly* what was coming next, and I was right.

The next scene is two years later. She is in medical school. She is brilliant and successful and sane.

Oh my God, I thought. That whole film. Her entire salvation. Her transformation from complete madness to sanity. It was my exact message. It was the transformative reality of deeper, ugly, unspoken truth!

Sure, the movie was about the birth of Psychoanalysis and Jung and Freud and blah blah blah, but it was also really simply about the healing power of telling the truth - the realest, darkest, most unthinkable, unspeakable (until it is spoken) truth! She didn't have to endure shock treatments, or a lifetime of commitment. She didn't need to be so heavily medicated that she couldn't put a sentence together.

She needed only to acknowledge her most shameful truth, which she had kept hidden her entire life - that she perceived herself as a disgraceful freak who had no place in this world.

Is Sabina's self-perception true, on the surface? Well, I guess that's a matter of personal opinion. Yet, is it really true to her beyond her own *JournalSpeak*? It appears not to be, as the movie plays out. Yet my point, our point my friend, is that it doesn't matter. At all. *The holding it down part was the madness, not the truth.* And although Sabina has challenges throughout her life, and lots of way inappropriate things happen between herself and Jung (none of which are even vaguely cool with me,) she is largely cured. She doesn't go batty again. In fact, she goes on (true story) to become one of the most influential female psychiatrists of our time. Potentially, of all time. That is, until the Nazis kill her for being Jewish. I digress. Moving on.

The shining point of this example is: Look at that! The healing power of truth can change one's entire life! It can be so ugly, so unthinkable. It certainly was, in this case. It wasn't very cool to be into sadomasochism at the turn of the century. Let's be honest - Sabina's admission that she was sexually excited, while being beaten as a child, naked, by her own father would be a difficult pill to swallow at any time in history. Yet she and Jung found the path and the strength to simply say it, out loud and to herself. And then miraculously, she was done with a dead-end life of institutionalization. She had never been clinically insane as every medical professional had believed. Instead, she was tortured to madness because she was drowning in her own shame.

Maybe your truth resembles Sabina's, to you. Or maybe it is something rather innocuous to society, yet you need to keep it hidden deep down within the polite nature that has been injected into your very sense of self. It could be something you swear you've excavated fully, yet somewhere in your heart you wonder if there isn't something else just beyond your reach. You might wonder about this because there remain portions of your life where you feel stuck, or anxious, or empty. Something is missing. Your pain is too great. This palpable acknowledgement often means that there is more truth to see, and be reckoned with.

I want you to know and remember: You can figure it out... it can be done. *You will be better.* Looking into the potentially ugly face of truth is literally the opposite of what you might imagine. You will not "hurt worse" by thinking about it. (More about this phrase later.) You will not become more stuck. Instead, the pain will lift out of your soul and your body, and you will finally understand that which you have been fighting so hard to repress.

You may need to grieve. We all need to mourn our painful truths, because they are ours. We've shared a long history with them. Once mourned, a space within you will be opened to forgive, both others and then, most significantly, yourself. And then, like Sabina, you will really live.

Example Number 3: *The Little Big Girl*

I want to tell you about Lucy. I offer you Lucy's story as another reminder of how ancient truths can rule us, until we unearth them and see ourselves and our lives in a different light. Lucy's tale, similar to all of our examples, also serves to fortify my point that we are all the same in our soft-n-chewy human centers. Lucy may not look like you or live like you, but if you can open yourself to her humanity you will feel akin to her. I will exhaust myself to convince you of this. I need you to embrace our sameness as human beings, because I need you not to be alone. That is, if you would really like to heal and grow as a human, and to release your pain. I want everyone on the planet to know this! Not to get all John Lennon on you, but...

Imagine. Imagine what the world would look like if people actually felt true empathy for one another without defense, and knew that they had all the power they needed to heal their own pain. Imagine all the people.

Lucy came to me because her closest friends and family were scared for her. They made her come. She was morbidly obese, and her body was aching in several places as a result of her weight and the strain it put on her whole system. Anyone could see it, and of course so could she. Lucy was clinically depressed, and currently unemployed. She had not had an intimate relationship in nearly 2 years. Not wanting to acknowledge the issues which were killing her, she thanked God often to anyone who would listen. Lucy preached often that she was blessed. She posted it constantly on Twitter and Facebook. It was clear to me however, that Lucy was suffering.

This is not about anyone's God. I love faith, and I love belief. In fact, spiritual people thrive the most in my practice, because faith in one facet of life begets faith in another. I do know however, that faith and belief struggle to rise to the surface in a human being, if they are being blocked by repressed truth. Here's why: You can preach, but if you cannot feel the depths of that which you espouse, the only person missing out is you. In Lucy's case, as she is just like any of us, she was terrified to be different or wrong or openly hopeless. So her best defense was to be maniacally grateful. Society is good with grateful, people are cool with it. They *like* it on Facebook.

I hear you, Luce. I know it feels right to say you're okay in a desperate attempt to be so, like you are being what everyone needs you to be. I also know that you are subconsciously caged in, and you don't feel confident that life is yours to own and change. The thing is, you can't be okay with the state of your life. Btw, I am not sitting here saying that it is inherently wrong to be overweight. You have to know this or you will miss my point entirely, and this potential moment of enlightenment will be wasted. I have known many fulfilled, genuine people whom society has deemed overweight, and they are living joyful, peaceful lives.

Here's the thing about Lucy: She was unhealthy, and I knew she was not fine with it. She was 34, moderately to severely depressed, unmarried, and living with her father and his wife. Lucy was not at peace. I could tell; it didn't take much detective work. For the first couple months of treatment we talked a lot about her day to day. We examined old boyfriends, jobs and friendships. After a while we arrived at a very important moment which I need to discuss with you. For best results, please remember to keep the following in mind, as you read:

Similar to Mikey, I know Lucy. I know her, because she has shown me. You need to remember this, because for the purposes of this example I have to jump about 30 steps ahead. I want to show you the power of what we discovered together. In real life this takes time, and this potentially lengthy process is necessary and normal. Every one of us needs our own time in order to be truly known, and in turn to know ourselves. I often think that it's not just the information that heals us… it's also our readiness to hear it.

Lucy and I were deep into a double session, discussing the end of her last love relationship two years prior. Lucy was telling me how it went down.

Luce:    We had gotten into a huge fight. He was such an asshole. He was being unfair and jealous, and yelling at me over the stupidest, insignificant crap. Like because a guy friended me on Facebook. I have never cheated on him. I had no interest in cheating, ever. I just wanted him to be nice to me, and treat me with respect.

Me:      So, what happened at the end that was so upsetting?

Luce:    I was on my computer at his place, and he saw that I had been friended by this guy. He lost it. He destroyed the room. He didn't hit me, but he went so crazy that I was seriously scared. He called me a cheater. I have never cheated on him! He was yelling such mean things at me. He threw his own books off the shelves. I didn't understand. I was so upset, I became silent. I just watched. I was in shock.

Me:      Once he calmed down, what happened?

Luce:    I had to go home. We needed to get to our jobs. I had no way to get there, 'cause my car wasn't at his house. He had to drive me. So we got into his car.

Me:      Was it terrible?

Luce:　　　No. It was okay. By then it was fine.

I sit, daily, across from you and hear you tell me that you are fine. I hate the word fine. Fine is the F-word in my practice. Do you feel fine, really? Is all of this, whatever it is, okay with you? Do you feel totally fucking great when someone is mean or insulting to you, or when you are invisible to people who should appreciate you? When you go completely unacknowledged by your closest loved ones?

Do you feel fine when somewhere inside, you know that you deserve more, or better? Sorry to sound like a psycho (but I am one, when it comes to this.) You simply cannot be fine when you are feeling these things. C'mon. Are you? No. Not really, right? The real question is: Why are you not fine?

~⁹

(Back to Luce and Me.)

Me:　　　What happened next?

Luce:　　　We were driving back home, in his car. He was over it, and he was starting to talk to me. Ya know, like about nothing. He was asking about work next week, and what we might do on the weekend. I was quiet. I wasn't answering anything, really. But I could tell, he was getting worse.

Me:　　　Worse?

Luce:　　　Yeah. You know... I was quiet, so he was getting madder and madder. I knew I had to lighten the mood, so I started answering back. I had to just be normal with him.

I am aware, because Lucy has been gracious and brave enough to share her life story with me, that in Lucy's history "lightening the mood" has not been light for her at all. She isn't focused on this fact at the moment, as she is fixated on a stressful memory of her ex-boyfriend, but I am. She will soon see this point clearly, as well. We're getting there.

For our purposes, allow me to give you an important piece of back-story which will prove central to your understanding in the end.

When Lucy was young, she lived with her mother who was very mentally ill. She wasn't ill the way one looks in the movies, or is portrayed in the media. She passed. This means that her illness often went unnoticed by people who didn't know her well. This common phenomenon often leaves children feeling unimaginably alone. Although Lucy's mother's condition was not obvious to the untrained eye, it wasn't hard for me to see it through Lucy's stories, and I knew what was going on.

I knew that her mother was suffering with a very damaging, long-term disorder. This will make sense to some of you: Her mother had a *Borderline Personality Disorder*. This is a disorder characterized by unpredictable and manipulative behavior and it is devastating for children to reconcile. It often remains hidden save the family members who are continually hurt, and many times they don't really know that their loved one is ill. They just think she's difficult and unreasonable. Lucy's mother seemed largely fine to most outsiders, until they really got to know her. As a child, this was confusing as hell.

When Lucy's self-worth was being shaped as a little girl, her mother was very disturbed. In addition to her personality disorder, she was in the throws of a Major Clinical Depression. She was, at times, suicidal. The worst part was that Lucy was virtually alone with her, accompanied only by her sister who was two years younger. Lucy took the brunt. Here is the most significant part: When Lucy's mother had her worst bouts with depression, she would lock herself away in her room. Prior to disappearing she didn't say much to her two little girls, save a couple of dramatic lines regarding life and death. She would then crawl inside, for days at a time.

Lucy was seven.

Lucy would lay on the floor, at her mother's locked door. She wasn't even sure, at times, if her mother was even behind the door anymore. She had no idea if she was dead or alive. She would lay with her mouth nearly touching the floor where there was a slight opening between the door and the carpet, and sing quietly. She would talk sweetly. She would stay there as long as necessary, talking and singing, until she "lightened the mood" enough for her mother to emerge from her cave to feed and care for her children. For little Lucy, this was necessary; *this was survival.* Lucy lightened the mood, and it saved her life and that of her baby sister.

That was then. This is now. Let's return to Lucy, today. Remember my whole rant about the mega-importance of linking one's past patterns to current struggles in order to find the deeper truth that heals? This is where we make sense of it all.

Although, with the help of other family members and loved-ones, Lucy had grown up to be a kind, intelligent and thoughtful woman, she was clueless about one very important truth: It was no longer a matter of survival to lighten the mood. It was no longer life or death. Actually, at this point in her life, lightening the mood when her boyfriend was emotionally abusing her was inflicting damage that she was unable to pinpoint. It was confusing the shit out of her.

Here is why the above is so critical: As we've discussed, truth lives on two levels: the surface, which is totally understandable yet keeping you stuck, and the deeper truth which heals amazingly, by allowing your seemingly insurmountable obstacles to melt away. The point of this reminder is that truth is relative. In fact, everything is relative.

Thank you, Albert Einstein. I have such a clear memory of one of the first epiphanies I ever had as a teenager about life. I overheard someone talking conversationally about Einstein's Theory of Relativity, and I was very thoughtful about it. I pondered, "What does this theory mean to me?"

I remember feeling enlightened (as enlightened as a teenager can be) to a truth of life, which at the time translated into: "If a baby drops a rattle from her highchair, she will cry and scream. This will seem silly to a grown-up. This is because the baby doesn't understand, in the moment, that someone can just pick it up and give it back to her! Her stage of development does not yet allow for such insight. Yet, the tragedy of the dropped rattle is real to her."

Here is the lightbulb teen moment.

"So... maybe the troubles that are torturing me currently, about my boyfriend, or my parents, or my homeroom teacher are all the same! Maybe, everything is simply relative. Maybe the fact that the stuff which seemed inconceivable as a 7-year-old which I now laugh over, can inform and console me a bit regarding what seems undoable now?!"

It was an immature understanding of the way everything is relative, but it was a beginning. I found it quite comforting, actually. I believe that this (profound for a teenager) thought sowed the seeds of my personal philosophy, my practice, and in time the writing of this book. So, if everything is relative, and our truths live within "everything,"

... then, so is truth! Truth is relative. Yes, yes it is.

Albert Einstein said, "We can't solve problems by using the same kind of thinking we used when we created them." This quote is perfect in my opinion to illustrate what we all need to understand in order to accept our truths, and mend our troubled minds to achieve greater peace in our lives. Einstein is often mistakenly characterized as solely a man of science, but he was actually a man of all humanity. Relativity is, in a roundabout way, the reason that Lucy had the healing epiphany of her life.

Lucy was subconsciously clinging to a relative truth as if it were absolute.

The fact that Lucy was reflexively lightening the mood was stealing her soul. It was robbing her of her voice. It was crushing her self-worth, and requiring her to hide under layers of fat.

Do you know why Lucy is dangerously overweight?

Lucy soothes herself with food because this behavior is a diversion created by her kind and loving brain in order to shield her from the pain that she cannot, without truth's insight, understand how to confront. She thinks she is safer worrying about something that she can control, however out of control this feels to her. Why? Because it feels less consciously painful to fixate on this problem of body image than to focus on the true devastating issue in Lucy's life. Let's translate this realization into *JournalSpeak*, with Lucy at the helm:

I have no voice. I surrendered it long ago as a result of my mother's illness, and my coexisting human need to be taken care of. I have no idea how to be heard without being scared to death that my words will be wrong, and will in turn lead people to abandon me.

I am even frightened to be quiet (which, at times would be true to myself) when others are angry, even when I am an innocent player. In the past, this damaging pattern has served to console and save me. Or, so I thought. As a result however, I have been enslaved within a lifelong need to lighten the mood, subconsciously, to save my own life. I had no idea that my life was no longer being protected; that in fact this precise misguided truth was slaying me. It was stealing my voice all over again.

Lucy came to understand, through our patient, consistent work, that she no longer needed to continue living her past patterns. She recognized, consciously, that she was no longer that little girl begging for her mother's care. She found the strength to look directly at these connected (past) issues that were paralyzing her in her current existence. She was able to admit out loud that she knew she had been eating to fill the space, to make herself feel numb for the moment. She'd actually been starving for attention and safety, and for years her brain had convinced her, "This hunger can be satiated."

As our dialogue progressed, Lucy was able to begin experimenting with having a voice. I told her: Let the world be your mirror. I wanted her to stop, temporarily, looking in the actual mirror to which she had grown accustomed, for her truth. I said: Speak your voice when you are ready, and see what happens. Use the responses of the world as your true mirror. She did, at first tentatively, and then again. The world responded. Family members reacted to her boundaries and self-expression more kindly than she expected. They changed their behavior and respected her more. Friends began to desire her company more often. Lucy herself, most importantly, began to shine a light that we could both see clearly. She saw beyond the wall of oppression that her relative truth had created, regardless of her best intentions.

Lucy is still persevering. She is a work in progress, just like me. Just like you. She will slide backwards at times, and then she will seek to comprehend why. As she understands each brief roadblock clearly, Lucy will then be able to embrace a fresh, evolved truth which will fortify and inform her of the next step in her process. We need not know the entire landscape of our futures; we need only do the next right thing for ourselves in the moment. It is the same for me, and I am here to tell you, it is the same for you.

I am so proud of Lucy. As human people, we can never see everything that lies before us; our destinies have yet to be created, by us and our places in the universe. All we can do is to live as purely as possible within our truths as effectively as we are able, in each of our moments. Upon each discovery of a truth, our next steps (whatever they might be,) will be bearable. When you consider how unbearable your own emotions and issues can seem sometimes, knowing this can be quite a consolation.

As for Lucy, she can now see and feel a tangible future. This is sometimes terrifying for her because it is filled with so much uncertainty, but it is clearer and brighter than any future she has ever imagined. It is her first vision of an empowered life that actually inspires her.

As of yesterday, Lucy has lost 36 pounds.

Example Number Four: *She Almost Gave Up For Good*

There are few stories more dramatic than Olivia's. I use her story often to inspire people. No matter how severe and complex one's pain, there is an answer and a cure in this work. I am forever changed having witnessed the severity of her struggle, and the valiant bravery with which she overcame it.

~

Olivia was 22 years old when her pain hit. When I use the word hit, it is purposeful, because her pain literally felt like a punch in the face. It was a time of change and flux in her life. Olivia had been accepted into a prestigious veterinary school and was finishing her undergraduate degree with honors, preparing to embark upon the rigorous four years ahead. With a passion for animals and animal welfare that is rare, Olivia had dreamed for years of becoming a vet and working around the world with exotic species, saving their lives and advocating for their causes. She was a perfectionist in every way; her long beautiful hair always in place, her body fit and slim, her grades straight A's and her boyfriend the Ken to her Barbie.

Olivia was solidly on her way to fulfilling her dreams. With vet school secured, she and her boyfriend Alex decided to move in together. He was working at the time in a city about 3 hours away and the long distance relationship was getting tiresome for them both. So, they decided, he would move to be with her in her college town. He had more flexibility, and was happy to make the sacrifice. And Olivia was thrilled… but there was conflict brewing beneath her lovely surface which was only the tip of the iceberg.

On the weekend Alex moved his things into her apartment, Olivia was stricken by a bad headache. Although she'd obviously had headaches before, this one was pretty severe, and she was disappointed that she couldn't be more helpful during Alex's move. As usual with her perfectionistic personality, she beat herself up badly, full of shame and regret that she had been such a disappointment. And although she felt those feelings, we now know that she didn't yet have the tools to *feel* as she needed to.

The headache became headaches, and the headaches were not just in her head - they were in her face. The pain grew stronger, and the throbbing and aching were coupled with a feeling of intense pressure, like there was an enormous weight pushing down on her face, her forehead, and the crown of her skull. The symptoms grew and grew in intensity, and finally Olivia had to surrender. She was hospitalized.

As Spring turned to Summer, it became clear that Olivia would not be attending veterinary school in the fall. One hospitalization led to another, as she was flown from state to state to see the best doctors in the country. Hospital stays lasted weeks, then months. She was subjected to every test, treatment, and medication available to modern medicine. Her diagnoses included Trigeminal Neuralgia, Acute Migraine Disorder, and finally New Daily Persistent Headache - a disorder with no cure.

For over a year Olivia moved from hospital to hospital, treatment to treatment. Vet school was deferred, with the hope that her symptoms could one day be managed adequately enough for her to attend. The best they could hope for, they decided, was to enroll her as disabled and utilize a notetaker and an aide. But at this point, even a scenario such as this seemed like a long shot of epic proportions. Olivia was in severe mind-numbing pain 24 hours a day. She had no ability to function on her own. She could get no relief from any medication. The treatments left her emaciated, and her hair began falling out.

Almost worse than the physical pain and fallout, was Olivia's mental health. It was completely broken. She was deeply depressed; helpless and hopeless. She had no more dreams of the future, and just stared into space as Alex and her parents lamented by her side. She didn't think she deserved their undying support, but she didn't even have enough energy to invest in insecurity. There was nothing left for her. Her spirit had died.

In an act of sheer desperation and a last impassioned effort to save her life, Olivia's tormented parents flew her to South Africa to participate in an experimental treatment which involved going in through her mouth and nose, and severing the nerves in her face and scalp. Olivia lived alone in Africa for several months, her family and Alex visiting when they could get away from their jobs and lives. Her face swelled and her hair continued to fall out. Her depression worsened. As it became clear that this treatment was not going to produce the desired results and lessen her pain to a manageable level, Olivia became suicidal and was returned to the states.

As she describes it to me now, "I came home to my mother's house, laid on her couch, and wished to die. There was nothing left for me."

With veterinary school an impossibility even with disability services and no ability to care for herself, Olivia needed to be watched around the clock to prevent her from taking her own life. This time of their lives was so dark, her parents still struggle to discuss it, years later.

Olivia's step-father Anthony, whom she adored and trusted, became acquainted with the work of Dr. John Sarno. After reading a bit of his writings, Anthony pondered that perhaps, *as crazy as it sounded*, Olivia's pain could be TMS. TMS stands for "Tension Myositis Syndrome." It is the diagnosis that Dr. Sarno coined, which is an umbrella under which all pain originating from emotional processes can be organized. When someone is diagnosed with TMS, it is understood that although the symptoms are as real as real can be, the origin of those symptoms is not structural, but emotional. There is no shame in this! It does not make your pain less genuine, destructive or unbearable. It is just another way to arrive at the same conclusion. Yet on this path, there is a path *out* that is profound. And I'm telling you once again, it will save your life if you let it. In Olivia's case, she was ready.

Olivia was ready to try anything. I mean, duh. Can you imagine this poor, sweet girl's life? So, with her mother, Anthony and Alex by her side, Olivia went to see another doctor - one of Dr. Sarno's associates in her city - to see if she was a candidate to treat her symptoms with Dr. Sarno's methods. The answer was a resounding YES. She should begin right away.

I met Olivia about a month later. By the time we made our acquaintance, she had already worked a basic therapeutic program with this physician, and her pain had come down to a manageable enough level that she was able to, independently, carry out day to day tasks. When her doctor referred her into my practice, it was April. We met via FaceTime, and she told me her story. I was silenced. Wow, this story was the worst one I had ever heard. She looked me in the virtual eye and said, "Is there any chance I can go to vet school in the fall? It's the only thing I've ever wanted to do."

Jeez.. I thought. Today was April. School started in late August.

"Yes." I told Olivia that day. "You will go. But can you fly here? I need you in person."

Olivia flew to me that weekend. She moved into the lovely boutique hotel in my office building, and we began our work. We had sessions for hours each day, starting early and working late, as I fit in every moment I could within my busy client schedule. I taught her everything I know, and she was a gifted and voracious student. She was fighting to save her own life; a battle to end all battles.

I explained to her what *JournalSpeak* meant, and I taught her how to translate her tapes into the deeper, emotional excavation that is only possible when one seeks her rawest truth. I shared my personal story with her. I told her with absolute certainty that she would be well, because I could see in her progress and her evolving understanding that she would. And she needed to hear that, because if you don't believe this process will help you, it cannot help you. Your perception is your reality, and Olivia did not perceive herself as being well. Yet as we worked, I could see that flicker of light in her eyes which I see every day in my clients - she was also beginning to perceive that maybe she wasn't that sick either. She was starting to believe that she might, juuust might, be able to recover from this literal hell in which she'd been living.

Olivia and I uncovered many truths in her courageous efforts. There was the fear about taking care of everyone else, at the expense of feeling her own feelings (a big one for us TMS sufferers,) which explained why her pain originated when it did. Alex's move, although joyous, was a huge trigger for Olivia. It infected her with the deepest conflict: Taking care of her own wishes and desires while being panicked that the other person is doing something just for her. We looked carefully, together, at her childhood. We uncovered how her parents' epically contentious divorce had turned her into a little girl who was constantly taking care of others at her own expense.

There were also the seeds deeply sown of her perfectionism, of both body and mind. We realized that perfectionism wasn't an irritating character trait for Olivia, but similar to Lucy with "lightening the mood," a survival mechanism so imperative that it was dictating every facet of her life. Her father had created an environment in his home following the divorce that was so rigid and shaming, that Olivia feared literal abandonment if she didn't live up to his impossible standards. Some might look at Olivia's problems as privileged ones, but TMS doesn't discriminate. She was not equipped to feel the pain that life inflicts on those of us who think our survival is only possible through perfection. If you think you're going to actually die, your brain has to do something to save you, and Olivia's crafty brilliant mind did a doozy on her.

Olivia returned home after a week, and we met via FaceTime regularly. She journaled, and she cried, and she broke down to me as often as she needed to. She began to learn that other people were safe too, and she slowly but surely began to trust that she could be less than perfect and still feel the love and acceptance of those closest to her. She took chances, and allowed the world to be her mirror. She drew real, solid boundaries with her family members who continued to hurt her. Not because she had to in order to heal, but as a measure born from her process. As we're going to discuss in just a minute, change flows naturally through the beauty of process. She didn't cut anyone out or do anything drastic, but she decided what she was worth, and she started to act on it.

Olivia's pain became less and less. She started to have days when she couldn't feel it at all. Those days got more and more frequent.

In the late summer of 2013, Olivia walked into veterinary school on her own two legs without a note taker or an aide. She aced that semester with straight A's - even though I kept yelling at her to make a fucking mistake here and there! The summer after her first year she traveled to Africa again, this time to work with a foundation that rescues and cares for elephants. She also spent time in Thailand with endangered species, and was the youngest veterinary student to be accepted into a summer internship at a prestigious emergency and referral hospital.

Her hair grew back, her body became strong, her mind became sharp again, and her spirit soared. In a million years, you would never be able to pick out that girl, swollen and skinny and sick in those weeks and months of hospital beds. Olivia is a force, who will absolutely make her mark in the field of veterinary medicine.

This summer Olivia will marry Alex, the love of her life.

~

OK! I'm feeling like we need to take a break from outlining Examples. I know that this is really heavy stuff, and it's a lot to take in. I'm beginning to worry about you. I need to tell you *It's a Process* before you get too overwhelmed.

# CHAPTER 9

## *It's a Process*

"Those who cannot change their minds
cannot change anything."
GEORGE BERNARD SHAW

Here is the deal: You are sitting here, today. The real and total you. You are reading this book, and hearing my examples. And, you are either:

A) In strong acceptance of the validity of my message, and tentatively curious (inspired, even?) about taking a look at your personal truths.
B) In basic acceptance of the validity of my message, but fearful bordering on skeptical regarding how this could ever apply to you, mostly because you struggle around how you might even begin to begin.
C) Kind-of-lost-and-vaguely-annoyed, but not ready to throw this book in the garbage.

or... And it's really you about whom I am most concerned.

D) Oddly checked out, far away, and withdrawn. If you were in my office, you might be averting my gaze. Perhaps you'd stop talking for a while, save a few polite responses to my questions. Maybe, you'd yawn?

Ok, you.

Here is why I am concerned: I fear that you may be checking out because you are unable to deal with the daunting task of even conceiving of truth in general, much less your own. This is not your fault. It is often a bi-product of living within one's tapes (your age-old stories) for so long that they are successfully, for the moment, masquerading as absolute truth for you. In addition, although it may sound crazy, when we become blocked in this fashion the defensiveness which we feel is actually our brains trying to protect us as our deeper truths begin to rise toward consciousness. As we have discussed, this cycle keeps us *safe in the unsafest way.* The end result of all this internal conflict is the thought which arises in one's head:

"This whole truth thing is bullshit, and not for me."

Hopefully if this is you, I didn't lose you 20 pages ago. If this is the situation of course, I'm just talking to myself. But just in case, let's assume for the moment that you are still hanging on. If so, this is probably due to the fact that although a good bit of skepticism has arisen in you over the last seconds minutes and hours, you are not ready to forsake your last ounce of...

hope.

I am writing this chapter to empower every one of you. Additionally, if you can relate to person D on the list, I am making my best effort to save you from yourself. Before you get too sensitive and throw me across the room for that, please take a listen to the following. We cannot hope for anything regarding truth's healing power, or pretty much any notion worth hoping for, without embracing and however dubiously welcoming our personal processes. Your *process* is the road to everywhere and everything you could've ever hoped for in your life up until this point. Unfortunately, so many of us misunderstand the concept of hope when it comes to bettering ourselves.

Without proper (read: true) understanding, hope can be a major roadblock in life.

"Whaaaat?" you gasp. (Then you can't help but turn to the random woman seated next to you at the coffee shop and say out loud, "The author of this book is seriously warped.") Well, maybe that's just what I'd be compelled to do... In any case, let me redeem myself immediately by making a lot of sense!

Hope, as defined, is a set-up. It is an impostor.

Hope is empty without the necessary tools to actually attain its promises. In order for hope to deliver on the comfort and motivation that we are taught to expect from it (as long as we hold on tight,) it must be interpreted through the lens of *process*.

The world's current widely-held definition of hope is, albeit unintentionally, tormenting each of us, every day. We are taught from childhood that if we can just "... keep our hopes up!" we will be rewarded with this almighty resilience to overcome any obstacle. But it doesn't go that way, does it? Did you know that countless people in our society perceive themselves as failures, often on several levels? This is because life is so full of experiences in which people's hopes and dreams fail to materialize as they'd hoped or dreamed.

Yet, if a person were to dare admit, "I have no hope," he might be deemed suicidal or at the very least, way pessimistic. Our culture all but shames people who admit to a deficit of hope; it is certainly not something very safe to say out loud. The natural conflict here is that society's widely accepted notion of hope is riddled with those damaging little expectations that injure and disappoint us each day. It's quite the conundrum. What do we do? Right? Do we hope and risk internalized self-hatred when 'less than everything' is delivered as we'd hoped, time and again? Or, do we forego hope altogether risking a life of misery and skepticism?

Don't get me wrong! I am a zealot when it comes to personal empowerment. It's just that most of us don't hope ourselves into power; we hope ourselves into a flushing toilet. If a person is not allowed to stop hoping without looking like a cranky-pants or worse, yet he still falls short of his goals too often with "no idea" how to remedy this pattern, how is he supposed to feel? I'll tell you. I'll tell you what we all feel like in such situations. We feel like shitty failing failures. But since we don't want to feel that tree falling in our forests, we *feel* mad at our kids, partners, co-workers, bosses, friends, dogs.

Let's do better. Let's look at this whole concept in a different light. Don't worry, I will turn myself into a pretzel to help and protect you. Reason: If you can accept and nurture yourself as a *work in process,* then you will not hit the wall of disappointment which keeps so many stuck after living through too many dashed hopes and expectations. If I can coax you onto the truth train, you will learn to honor your personal process like the most precious gift; you will hold it as tightly as a security blanket. This security blanket is the one I want you to cherish. It's the only one that can set you free.

The reason why it is so important to hash out this whole hope thing before we dive right into your personal process is that in truth, hoping or waiting for anything within your process can really slow things down, or even cause you to give up on yourself. I know it's so hard to unlearn patterns that you've always practiced, but adjusting your thinking on this one will bring you more relief than you might imagine.

Whatever hope might mean to you, the beautiful part is: It's just not necessary here! Once you've embraced the notion of a more fulfilled, less conflicted existence through living your truth, the concept of hoping for something simply doesn't exist. The energy of your process, whether joyous or difficult at the moment, surrounds you and feeds you. You don't hope for it; you just live it. If you're willing to consider this possibility, then let's go further.

Everyone should be listening very carefully now. We are about to address a very super important part of the book right here.

Life is a journey, right? I know you've heard that one, with all the business about there is no destination, and don't waste your life waiting to arrive some place. Obviously, these two statements are undeniably true. (Just go with it.) Here's one that is even better and more super-duper true: There is no such thing as wanting to be happy. How many times have you heard a friend, or your partner, or a TV personality, or your teenage daughter whine, "I just want to be happy!"

Happiness is not a permanent state of being, my pet. It is dynamic.

Happiness is a moment. It is many, infinitely varied moments. Perhaps you've had lots of these moments; perhaps it's been a long while since you could identify even one, clearly. Either way, no one in the world is *happy*. The same goes for sad or angry or scared or ashamed, etc. Think about it. During your happiest times, were there not moments in the days that felt sad and/or defeating? Of course there were. The same goes for sadness. Not one sad (even clinically depressed) person could convince me that he or she was able to ignore every moment of surprising levity, or personal connection that brought joy, however fleeting.

Everything we are, and we feel, exists in moments. Such is life.

The same is true of truth. Truth is certainly not a destination, and I venture to say that not one human is done embracing her truth until she draws her last breath. Each nugget of our truths is revealed to us as we are ready, and/or our insightful work creates readiness within us. Whether this book makes total sense to you, or simply leaves you with an irritating curiosity, you are getting a sense of where you are in your process. The experience of reading every word of this book matters. The experience of every conversation it sparks, or exploration it ignites, even the frustration it manifests, matters. In other words, *It's a Process.*

If you were my actual client reading this, you would be wearing a sly smile and either rolling your eyes, shaking your head with a grin, or nodding emphatically - this is all depending on where you are in your personal process. The reason this phrase calls upon such diverse emotions, is that the process itself is a source of both blinding frustration and euphoric enlightenment, and everything in between. The first milestone of your process is acceptance. This means acceptance that real healing can only be accomplished through living out whatever process lies ahead of you through the excavation of truth. It means accepting, with loving kindness for yourself, that you must allow yourself to trod as patiently as necessary through your crap, toward each truth along the way.

What we are doing will not only take time, but will require a abundance of intrinsic patience and kindness. In the spirit of Portia Nelson's *Autobiography in Five Short Chapters* referenced earlier, each chapter - some longer than others - will need to be tolerated until you are ready to move past it. Not just any person... you. I can love you to the ends of the earth and back, and I can't make it go any faster. Trust me, I wish I could. Every damn day! I wish it could go faster for me in my own process, but I know too much now. I know that there is no way out, other than through. And we all must go through at our own pace. As Winston Churchill said, "If you're going through hell, keep going."

However, we must recall the oh so important comforting piece: The uncovering of deeper truth is the exact path out, which means you will eventually be out of each jail, free of everything that is currently holding you hostage. Translation: it's going to be okay. It will, if you can find the bravery to release the safety nets of your tapes and your patterns. It might feel shitty for a little while as you get used to the chilly waters of your process. After all, it's been a while since you've taken off the cloaks of defensiveness, entitlement and being right.

Yet I must tell you, I've seen people transform countless times. I've lived it within myself. The enlightenment along the way is real, and the healing is enduring. Without the obligation to divert you from seeing and feeling your ugly truths, your brain has no choice but to be your champion instead of your adversary. You will have partnered with it, and it will express its relief and gratitude by forgiving you of your _____ (pain, resentment, inability to act, paralyzing fear, self-doubt, self-hatred, debilitating patterns and disorders, etc.) It's your blank to fill in. You know the answer.

We now arrive at a point where I'm sure that my clients will smile, regardless of their potentially tiresome processes. I will share a phrase which has become quite the language of our work. I say it, because it is true. I preach it, because you need to hear it, regardless of the process you've got going on. The sooner you integrate what I am saying here, the closer you will be to uncovering your magical ability to fit the key that you already possess into the lock of each personal jail, and throw open the door.

*Life is not good or bad, happy or sad. Life is about choosing between what hurts, and what hurts worse.*

Take a minute. Take it in. Sounds horribly negative, right? Sounds like a bitter old witch, stealing your shot at happiness and replacing it with cynicism. I know. I don't like the thought of it either. Here's the thing, though.

It's true. And it's such a relief.

I can't tell you how often I sit across from a human, a You, and we are talking about your life, and I can see clearly that you are struggling to embrace the concept at hand. You are hurting, and waiting, and desperately trying... for happy. Or okay. Or good. Or settled.

Let's pretend for the purposes of the moment that you are my client - the woman we discussed in Chapter 5 who is having an affair and completely distraught over her many conflicts. You are dissatisfied with life in several ways, yet you cannot bring yourself to un-dig your heels regarding your protective certainties, which serve only to paralyze your life. I feel for you and I understand you, because we are all the same. The situation may differ, but we all ache. When we suffer, we all suffer the same.

I need to help open your eyes, so you can save yourself. Let's look at you again now that we've come this far, and our understanding about truth and process is far deeper and more meaningful.

Remember - This is a raw summary of our interaction, personal niceties removed, for the purposes of this dialogue:

So, you feel unhappy in your marriage. Right, I completely hear you. It sounds like your husband's really unfair. He blows up at you. He takes his personal crap out on you, and your kids. I know the kid part kills you the most. He has lied to you, and you have found out. When he asks you to change, and you do, he discounts it by finding another issue to complain about. I hear you.

There's another version of this story, however. The interesting part is that it's not his side. I am also hearing this version from you. It's the other side of *your* story.

You want to be married. Not just to anyone...to him. He's the father of your children. You're not that attracted to him anymore, but you realize this could be a result of your history together. Maybe this could change if you guys could learn to communicate? You respect him as a person, when you can let go momentarily of your anger and sadness. You see his flaws, and even though you've suffered within them many times, you still want him beside you. He is trying, but he is driving you crazy. Mostly because you can see that he still loves you too, but he's too blocked to live it. He's existing in the world of his bullshit pride and the many years of sustained damage at the hands of his own parents. All of this makes you feel confused. It feels miserable, yet you can see him, and you still want him. Your state of frustration and isolation have led you to make a choice of which you are ashamed: you have been unfaithful. You hate yourself for it, and you are conflicted and sad.

You sit across from me and lament, "What should I do?" I am patient and understanding, as I am human right there with you. Your story may not be mine, but I have known pain and conflict. I understand confusion; everybody understands confusion. We take our time. I make sure the whole story is laid out in front of us. Then, when I know that we can see the whole picture, I break the news that you don't necessarily want to hear, yet I know you need to hear:

Life is not good or bad, happy or sad. Life is about choosing between what hurts, and what hurts worse.

Of course, I can't tell you whether or not to stay with your husband. *You* can of course, as you live out your process. On the first day that you walk into my office, you may have no idea what to do. On the other hand, you might "know" that you could never leave. You're sure. You couldn't survive alone, obviously. Or conversely you, "Cannot live with this shit for one more minute! It's unacceptable to have the kids experience this. You are out!"

In either case, you may feel certain of what is, and what is not. "That's cool," I say. You are at the beginning of this specific process in your life. We'll see where it takes us. One thing's for sure, though; the only certainty I will absolutely agree to: "It" will change, whatever "it" is. It will change several times in fact, before you can say with actual peace that you know what you need, and in turn, what you need to do.

In the case of the dilemma at hand, there are two choices. Stay, or go. "Stay" has a list underneath it of things which will be realities if you stay. They may change over time with the help of personal growth on either of your ends, or they may not. "Go" has another list which may seem equally unpalatable. Here's the deal though: It's not. It's not *equally* unpalatable. It's either more, or less... today. Tomorrow it may change, but today is the only day we are dealing with. Today you have a choice between what hurts and what hurts worse, and today you've made a choice.

Here's where you get stuck, though: It feels like there is a third option. It feels like there is an option of, "Stay but he will change and I will change the way I feel enough to be cool with staying and he won't be so argumentative and I won't be so angry and everything won't feel so hard all the time." On a related note, there is another third option that tempts you: "Go but it won't be that bad financially and I won't be that lonely or regretful and the kids will be fine and I won't worry about them and it won't be that hard to be dating again and I'll be totally cool with the decision."

Neither one of those options exists. Here's what does. There are some sucky things about staying, and some sucky things about leaving, and one of them sucks less. And that one is the one you're choosing to do today. And it's okay, because you only have two options, so today you can forgive yourself for choosing that one, even though it hurts.

Because things hurt in life, and if you expect them not to, or for things to be easier than they are, you will remain stuck forever.

Each day is a new day. I have a Buddhist saying written on the wall of my bedroom. It reads, "Each morning we are born again. What we do today is what matters most." So, know that whatever you are choosing today is just for today. It does not box you in, or take away your power to change your mind. But if you constantly wait and hope for a third, easier option to present itself, you will never come to peace with your current choice. Hoping for the third option is the recipe for stagnation.

Your process is defined by your choices. You only need to choose one small thing at a time; the next right thing for you to do. This is the striking beauty of process. It is not hinged on hope, or expectations. You need only live it passionately, and the rewards of truth, clarity and peace are the natural bi-products.

There is always a *hurts* and a *hurts worse* for each of us, in every situation. I say this emphatically because you have unique needs. Although we share a human essence, one person can tolerate years of emotional disconnect as long as she can spend all the money she wants, and have the freedom to make personal choices which matter to her. The woman next door can sustain emotional disconnect for only a very brief period of time before it drives her mad; money be damned! One man might be fine sacrificing the best sex of his life for a long-term relationship which makes him feel safe, the way his parents didn't. A similar looking man across the hall would rather die than live out his days without passion. We are complicated creatures, us humans. The salient point of this particular moment is this:

Peace = Living your process.

Accept the need to look at your life. Understand your motivations. Discover, and gently embrace your nature. Make friends with the parts of yourself that are so tied to your nature, you know they couldn't sustain change. Nurture the aspects of yourself which make you uncomfortable. They are still part of you, and need a place to reside.

It is only through your process that you can learn, with confidence, that which hurts and that which hurts worse for you in any given situation. You will then be able to begin the next chapter of your autobiography, again and again. It will always be both exciting and daunting, painful and passionate. Yet whatever it is, it will also be true. And within excavated deeper truth, there is no need for hope, or regret.

Now, let's do this shit.

# CHAPTER 10

# How

"If you hold a cat by the tail, you learn things
you could not learn any other way."
MARK TWAIN

S o, here we are. You, and me. And we've arrived, right? We've arrived at how.

"Finally!" you might think, "I've been listening carefully for many pages, and I've been trying my best to understand. I'm ready to hear exactly how to do this for me."

Or perhaps, you naughty thing.

You bought this book and skipped directly to this page. You saw the word how and you hopped right on over. Maybe you thought, "Let me see if I can just get it without having to read all the other blah blah blah. I'm not patient like other people. Hopefully this will be enough to help me." This concept totally cracks me up, because I've done stuff like that a million times. Sometimes it has worked for me, relatively, and other times it has left me wanting and eventually re-reading. In any case, if this is you then I will simply invite you in. Go for it! Read along with us. My sincere opinion is that you will get so much more from this experience if you read the story from the beginning. It might look like an instruction manual, but this book is really raw humanity - mine and yours - and you can't fast forward through that.

Having said this, I know by now that I can't make you do anything you don't want to do. I've learned this by observing myself, so how can I blame you? So, give it a go if you'd like. Maybe, afterwards, you will choose to start from the start.

~

So... how.

A very smart grad school professor for whom I have deep admiration read an earlier draft of this manuscript and said to me, "Have you ever heard of the book, *The Answer to How is Yes*, by Peter Block?"[6] I hadn't at the time, but the title alone meant so much to me the moment I heard it. Those six words seemed to embody everything that I'm trying to explain in this effort.

Translation: I can tell you how. I certainly know how I discovered my initial deeper truths, with the guidance of my unbearable back pain and Dr. John Sarno. I operate a thriving private practice where I walk people through healing from their pain every day. There is a method for journaling and therapeutic practice that facilitates a very effective commencement on your truth journey. I'm gonna tell you every secret I know. The value it has added to my life is priceless.

When my clients beseech me, with a world of longing in their eyes, "Please just tell me how to do this," the same response arises in me, again and again:

"You're doing it, honey!"

In my office, I am so tuned in to you that we, together, live within the constant patient maneuvering down the rocky river of your process. I can't, however, get away with that answer here with you. I can't be in the room with every one of you, and from my current seat it is impossible to have a good handle on what you are doing or how you feel about it. Here, I need to be more specific. After all, the whole point of this book is to help you.

We live in a society addicted to outcomes. We bring our cars in to be fixed, and they return fixed. When we test positive for strep at the doctor's office she gives us antibiotics, and when we take them we get better. We dedicate ourselves to exercise in order to strengthen our bodies, and if we are consistent, we see results. These things are all fine and good. They keep us safe and comfortable, and allow us to accomplish tasks in life. Loveliness.

In the world of your mind, heart and soul, however, there is no such thing as an outcome - not really. Even if we postulate that results from psychotherapy are positive outcomes (which of course I support - I'm a psychotherapist!) there is a distinct difference between our world of tangible outcomes and the persistently better mental health of an individual in therapy. A person in therapy is on a journey. I am highlighting this because I have seen many people delay their journeys significantly by striving to be "done," or desperately waiting to be better.

Since one's process is not outcome-driven, these people will (either subconsciously, consciously, or both) feel like failures, similar to the whole hope debacle. This will not do! So I say to you, my lovely human: Please try not to equate growth in this process with any sort of outcome, or convince yourself that healing will resemble an arrival.

Instead, open yourself to the possibility of possibilities. Invite yourself in, and be kind and loving to your new guest. Create the space and freedom to learn who you actually are; not your mom's version, or your sister's. The last gift I will hand you before I shove you out of the nest into the universe of How, is this: Human suffering resides in the gaps that we create between seeing our deeper truths, and letting action naturally flow from that.

Translation: Human beings don't need to seek *change*, regardless of how we are convinced otherwise by our outcome-addicted culture. We need only to open ourselves to seeing our truths. Once we can clearly see ourselves and our situations without judgement, change will occur effortlessly, as appropriate for each of our lives. This is truth to me, as it will be to you, someday. Don't worry.

# HOW

The first step in how is understanding and embracing the messages contained in the previous pages of this book. If you don't get it, then you can't believe it can help you. If you don't believe it can help you...it can't help you. Complete acceptance of what I say, at this moment, is not required. Just come armed with a big dose of willingness and an open mind. If you are struggling with acceptance, yet you can agree to suspend your disbelief for the time being, you will allow in some room to begin your journey. I believe that you will find the proof you are seeking within your process, after a little while. For the purposes of this moment we are going to triumph and posit that not only do you get it, but you are willing (however haltingly) to believe it. Fine, then. Let's talk how.

Whether you are natural writer at heart or not, you can heal effectively within a journal if directed properly. I have worked with an array of people more diverse than the most complicated prism, and every single one of them has released pain effectively after becoming acquainted with translating routine bitching and moaning to *JournalSpeak*. I firmly believe that the most effective way out of your brand of pain is journaling. It is the simplest and most direct way to inform your conscious brain what your subconscious mind is brewing.

Journaling is an age-old method of healing, and although as a society we have come to place much more confidence in a pill or a surgery or a treatment of sorts, those who journal regularly can tell you that there is no greater way to know yourself, find your truest answers to life's dilemmas, and sooth your most troubling emotions. Essentially, I see journaling as a way to say anything you damn well please as if you are winning every argument in your life with every person with whom you struggle, and feel as heard as if it all took place. Actually, way more.

Don't be deceived into thinking that there is power in winning an argument. I am here with a wealth of human experience to tell you that categorically there is not. Being right is a ruse of epic proportions. You think you've won, when in fact you've almost certainly deluded yourself into a corner, as being right is being all alone. You think your opinion is based on the highest order of truth. But in fact your opinion is not just of the moment; it is a complicated combination of the situation at hand as filtered through the lens of your history, experience and emotional triggers. You are so sure. I'm here to tell you that you will hurt worse if you stand on ceremony.

Your journal is your place to explore, and to heal. Have the argument. Throw down in a way you'd never have the nerve to do in person. Say horrible, hurtful, unthinkable things. Blame, judge. Be 13 again, be 6 again… be honest. Forget about what you should or shouldn't say. Tell your daughter you're jealous of her, your husband you're no longer at-tracted to his fat gut, your best friend that she's too petty for words. I'm gonna tell you a little secret that I promise will prove true for you in your journey: Once you say it, you often don't feel it anymore. And then more will be revealed. A lot of times, ultimately it's about you. And then you don't have all that pesky clean-up necessary with real arguments.

Personally, writing it down saved my life. I had to relax my brain and my overwhelming guilt of admission, and reveal my surface, acceptable, obviously upsetting experiences first. I wasn't aware at the time that my deeper truths would arise somewhere down the bunny trail which began at each of these socially acceptable truths. I now know that most people need to start with "safe" in order to go deep.

Let's walk through it, together.

First, as Sarno's work suggests I made three lists.[7] I believe that this is the best place to begin. I took a piece of paper and divided it into three sections, like this:

| Childhood | Daily Life | Personality |
|---|---|---|
|  |  |  |
|  |  |  |
|  |  |  |

I made lists under each heading, in a bulleted fashion. Each bullet meant something to me. No one else needed to get it, which made it much easier to punch out. Here is a small sample of what my lists looked like, after a bit of effort:

| Childhood | Daily Life | Personality |
|---|---|---|
| The time with the essay (6th grade.) | Motherhood - two babies and tired/spent. | I need to do everything perfectly, or I'm a failure. |
| The dinner at my cousin's sweet 16. | Marriage - feeling alone. | I'm not comfortable unless everyone likes me, all the time. |
| Moving, all the time. | No job, no purpose. | I want to please everyone. |
| Dad helping me with HW. | Money. | I don't like to be in places with people who "all know each other," and I'm the odd man out. |
| M&D's second separation. | My friend (blank) and the way she makes me feel bad. | I feel alone, even in a crowded room. |
| My first new bicycle (3rd grade.) | Why is everyone always "OK," and I'm not? | I never feel proud of myself, even when I "know" I should. |

In the *JournalSpeak* Chapter, I detailed the meanings behind these three headings in reference to conquering my back pain, and I don't want to bore you by repeating them. Just know that if you need any clarification about why each list is important and what kinds of items should be included, you can flip back there.

When I first created these lists, the bullets that were included encapsulated as much of my life's pain and damage that I could currently identify. I patiently took each item, put it at the top of a piece of paper or a blank document on my computer which remained unsaved and then deleted, and I free wrote without pressure. As I wrote, I followed my mind's natural path down the unforeseen trails which ensued.

Although each train of thought commenced with an upsetting event or frustrating personality trait from one of my lists, I quickly realized that my deeper healing truths were often separated by quite a distance from the originally identified issue. For example, the healing truth that I felt hatred of being a mom, and then of myself (which morphed quickly into deep sadness for my misguided innocent childhood defenses,) began with the simple heading of "Motherhood." That particular truth healed me immensely, and I never would've known it had I just played my tapes on repeat. My back pain, at the time, was the direct result of my body's reflex to hold down the real truths which I didn't even know about consciously. Those truths arose because I put my trust in the process, which let me relax into the experience and allow my defenses to fall away. I took comfort in the fact that no one was listening but me, and the life that I was saving was my own.

I examined each item on those lists in no special order, but felt free to change direction as any of them popped out at me. *I carved out about 30-60 minutes a day, for me.* This is so important. I know it feels like a long time to take out of your day, but if it will literally cure you of your pain, isn't it worth it?  If it will bring you to a level of peace that you have yet to experience, can't you find the time?

For me, sometimes it was all at once; sometimes it was 30 minutes in the morning and 30 in the evening.  As I felt ready, I put each and every bullet from my lists on the top of different pieces of paper, unsent emails and word documents, and I wrote.  I wrote, and I cried, and I thought, and I wrote.  I lit up when my truths pleasantly surprised me - the kind of delighted little secret smile only possible when one is in the presence of raw, beautiful truth.  Many times I would end up in stunned yet comfortable silence after a journaling session.  I was in awe, of myself.  For a person who more often than not leans in the direction of her flaws, this was an interesting exercise in itself.

Each page started like this:

| **Motherhood** |
|---|
| I'm exhausted.... (my) blah.... |
|  |
|  |
|  |

Remember.  Your first seemingly obvious list items may not be, on the surface, the truths that heal.  However, they need to come first; they need to be the *X marks the spot*, so that you have somewhere to dig.  For me, the Motherhood page began (recall the JournalSpeak Chapter):

"C'mon!  What parent of a toddler and an infant is not tired?  Who among us is immune to frustration?  What kind of person never complains?"

Translation: "I can easily say the socially appropriate stuff about being a new mom; the stuff people hear all the time." In my mind, if someone overheard me saying this to a friend at the grocery store, she'd be on my side even if she'd never met me before. I personally really needed that safety.

I needed to start there so I could feel supported by the world in general, in my frightened perception. I was desperate to be forgiven for my failures by the nameless/faceless mass of people who had been judging me my entire life, even if only in my mind. I required this step, so I could eventually stumble bravely down the path to truth, and eventual peace. My necessary healing truths at that moment were unacceptable and inaccessible to me, and my dear protective brain. I needed some breaking-in first.

Our lists are a great beginning. They, alongside our courageous digging efforts, can reveal the truths necessary to heal. The most important, self-protective thing to remember when you attempt your own *JournalSpeak* is this: No one should read your written thoughts, unless you explicitly decide to share them. That's why you erase your writings, or rip pages of paper and toss them in a safe place, not the kitchen garbage can. This is not a journal that you need to re-read, trust me. Once you come to each big (Eureka!) moment, you will not forget it. And even if you do, momentarily, it doesn't matter. The exercise itself is what frees your pain, not the meaning you make of it. In other words you will *see*, and as you integrate that which you see, one by one your walls of pain will tumble down gently without conscious effort.

In my personal experience and in my practice, there is no way around starting with the easy surface stuff. You need to be safe. Hence, you need to either write, or say, or think:

"I'm not that bad. I'm lovable! I do the right things. I am good. I am not a disappointment. I make the right choices. I am in charge of myself. I love my kids, (of course I do!) My life is fine. My parents have always loved and approved of me, the best they could. They know I'm a success. I believe in God, without question! I'm satisfied with my life. After all, that's life, right? I can take the punches. I can look on the bright side! Time will heal what ails me. It's fine. I'm cool... It's all good."

I totally get you. I hear you. I lived that way for quite a while, and so does everyone. I just need to say this once more, for the last time, I swear. Well, kind-of... maybe. Whatever.

This kind of talk will not heal you. It will keep you stuck, forever.

Here's freedom - in *JournalSpeak*, of course.

"I feel like I am bad, and I don't quite know why. I worry that I am unlovable. I never do the right things (I have my mom in my head.) I will never be good enough. I am a disappointment. I make the wrong choices all the time. I am rarely in charge of myself. I love my kids (of course I do!) yet sometimes I also really can't stand them. Sometimes, I actually wish they were never born. My life is unmanageable. My parents have always disapproved of me. I feel like a baby admitting this, but I know they think I'm a failure. The worst part is, secretly, I agree with them. I try to believe in God, but sometimes I don't feel clear at all. I can't seem to see my faith with certainty, the way everyone else does. I'm secretly, shamefully, ragefully dissatisfied with my life."

"I hate when people say, "That's life." I hate everyone. People think they know everything! I've taken enough punches. I'm sick of acting OK when I'm not. I have enough character for a stadium full of people. I just want easy for once. Trying to look on the bright side makes me feel less than people who actually can! Time hasn't seemed to heal much, and I don't understand that. Everyone says it should. Obviously something is wrong with me. It's not fine. I don't feel fine at all. In fact, I so rarely feel as good as I think I should."

If human people could say this brand of stuff, simply to themselves without the fear that it might plunge them into despair, because it will not, then they might begin to understand the ways in which seeing oneself can converge with many facets of personal peace. Perhaps they'd embrace the concept: Once we see our truths and ourselves clearly, healing isn't an effort. It's a given.

Remember, not one detail of your life needs to change in order for this process to heal your pain. If change becomes the reality, it is always born of your process. You don't have to alter your personal situation, or your job. You don't need to confront anyone who has damaged you. At times, when personal growth allows people to see their deeper truths clearly, the natural flow of their journeys are toward change. However I want you to feel safe in the knowledge that you don't need to change your cozy little life, ever, unless you choose to do so. You are the master of your life. Perhaps you've forgotten.

There is so much beauty and peace down the road and around the corner, my friend. Truth can offer so many gifts, and so much relief. I have personally witnessed a world of forgiveness, of others and ultimately, of myself.

Once you begin to live the gift of this process and the shifts which become evident within you, you will not feel like a victim anymore. I promise.

Very simply, you just need the courage to really, rawly, be true with yourself: What is your role in this drama you call life? What do you feel, even if it is impolite bordering on mortifying? Take a walk to a quiet place, and surrender. Rip out and trash the pages afterwards. Who gives a shit? Go to the Starbucks in the next town over with your legal pad of paper. Scrawl all over it while you spend 20 bucks on over-priced coffee drinks, and then shred it into the public garbage can down the street. Bring your laptop, type into an email with no one as the recipient, and then never send. Delete the draft. Keep yourself safe, as *JournalSpeak* will not be understood by a human who doesn't speak the language, but stop being scared.

You're not safe that way, either.

Do you need more human guidance? No worries. That's fine! You can solicit support from friends or take the hand of a therapist along the way, if that makes you feel more comfortable (See Appendix B.)

Just stop sweating the small (big, frightening) stuff. Stop sweating all the garbage that you've been programmed to sweat. Trust me, it's not working for you. Bottom line: This is your choice. This is your life - the only one you will get. It is yours to survive, yet miraculously it is also yours to change.

You will uncover the actual weight of the massive burden you've been carrying. Upon this realization, this *seeing*, your emotional load will be oddly suspended... hanging in the universe, forever swirling in the energy of shared humanity. Call me crazy! I'm sure one of you will. But maybe... just maybe, one of you won't.

C'mon, you. Let's be lighter. Let's let go of our burdensome crap. Let's see what is left of this stupid little life.

# CHAPTER 11

# Patience and Kindness and Forgiveness

"Friendship with oneself is all important,
because without it one cannot be friends
with anyone else in the world."

ELEANOR ROOSEVELT

T his is not easy. Truth is not the path of least resistance. In fact, it is likely the path of most resistance for your evolving brain which thinks it's protecting you. Yet, you cannot let this deter you. I have the final piece of the puzzle right here. It will help you in this great, difficult quest. It will forgive you when you feel defeated. It will lift you when you feel exhausted. And you need it; everyone needs it.

Patience and kindness, for *yourself.*

I am going to give you credit, and imagine that you know what it feels like to have patience and kindness for another human. I am also going to judge you, and postulate that you feel it far less often for yourself. This needs to change. Our whole truth thing will never work without these imperative ingredients in the recipe.

~

So, you hate your kid sometimes. You're jealous of your best friend, to the point of inner rage. You're sure everyone has it better than you. They have it all figured out, but you don't. Fat or thin, you still feel unattractive. You're never good enough. It's your parent's fault. No, it's your husband's fault. Actually, it's your sister's fault. Your parents always loved her more. Yeah, but what sucks the most is that the resulting feelings still reside in your lap. You can't just be angry, or bitter, or resentful anymore. Ugh. It's so annoying.

If you sit with that and that alone and go no further, you will feel terrible. You will feel so terrible! Of course. You will say, "What the hell, Nicole? What's the point of this crap?"

Then I will say, "One more minute, kid. Just drink this magic potion and you will be just fine."

Out of the darkness and into the light. Ok, let's go. If you are over 21 it is likely that you've done a shot in your life. Let's say tequila quick and dirty, followed immediately by sucking a lime. The lime makes all the burn go away. It cools your mouth and throat. It makes everything muuuch better.

So here, right now, is what you need to do... what you must do. I know you can do it, I have faith. Tell your truth, without fear. Tell it, and write it, to yourself alone, or to your chosen support system, or to your therapist. And then chase it, immediately, with patience and kindness for yourself:

> You might be flawed, but so are we all. You might have been unloved, but that doesn't mean you are unlovable. You might hate your kids at the moment, but you are just a human person! Every single one of us who is brave enough to say it, hates them sometimes. No matter your truth, there is no right or wrong for you, if you see yourself as a member of the human race. Whatever it is, someone else out there is feeling it too, right at this very moment. *Every action has an origin, and every origin is understandable.* Regardless of how ugly it looks to you, it is forgivable with a patient and kind perspective. If we could cherry-pick a bunch of "yous" out of society, you would have good company. We all suffer the same. We are all, actually, in it together. We just don't remember that all the time.

We all, quite simply, just want to be forgiven.

Forgiveness is a concept that cannot be downplayed. We ache for forgiveness, from everyone, even from people who've hurt us more than we've hurt them. My greatest example of this has been my father. As a child, my father was extremely critical of me, caught in the grips of his own issues. This is clear to me now, but as a young child I felt like I was never enough, and became plagued with a need to achieve and exceed with the hope of being acknowledged by the world at large.

This struggle served me well in many ways, but the hole in my heart and the impossible task of being enough has stolen peace from my soul and my serenity. Although I didn't do anything to wrong him by not being a perfect specimen, the child in me still felt like a disappointment. Adding insult to injury, my father died when I was just 27 years old, so any healing conversations we might have had as two adults were silenced. I was walking around feeling like a failure despite my many successes; there was something missing that I couldn't understand.

I realized that I needed to forgive myself, but somehow I couldn't bring myself to do so. What was stopping me? What was missing? It came to me. I couldn't forgive myself until he forgave me. Not because logically I was to blame, but because there was a little girl still alive within me who couldn't believe that she was good enough, and who needed to say she was sorry.

I needed to be forgiven first by him, *in JournalSpeak,* for being such a disappointment. Remember that JournalSpeak doesn't always make logical sense. Why should a child doing her very best to find her way, owe an apology to an unreasonable adult acting out his own deficits on her little self? In the real polite world of our surface truths, she doesn't. But we need to honor the fact that the little child still lives in each of us, until we give her a voice and help her to find peace. Although I didn't actually owe my father an apology, I was living in many ways continuing to act out the need for approval left over from my relationship with him.

So, I allowed myself to be that kid for just a moment, with the maturity and insight of an adult. I needed to clear away the wreckage of those misguided judgments which shaped my childhood self, and in turn my current world view. Of course, I was not actually a failure. But

I felt like one, and my perception was my reality. I channeled my best *JournalSpeak* translation guide, and I spoke in my journal to my father:

> Daddy, please forgive me. I'm sorry that I had the wrong interests. I'm sorry that I didn't ask the right questions. I'm sorry that I never seemed to make you happy enough. I didn't mean to hurt you. I always wanted to please you. I wish I could've been smarter. I wish I could have been the kind of kid you wanted. I'm sorry I'm sorry, i'm sorry i'm sorry...

I sobbed and sobbed, and I felt him forgive me. Maybe it was him, and maybe it was just that piece of myself which has grown into a confident woman who knows who I am. Either way, I was stricken with the power of forgiveness. We all simply want to be forgiven. Maybe it looks like we are angry, or depressed, or racked with pain on the outside. But scratch the surface of any of those feelings, and there is fear. Fear that we aren't good enough, usually as a result of childhood experiences.

Once I tapped into the forgiving energy I needed to feel, which arose from giving that little girl a voice and allowing her to stop being defensive, I was able to begin forgiving myself. Forgiveness is a process as much as anything else we've discussed here, so I am still on that journey. But I can't tell you enough about the value of being brave; looking at forgiveness in a broader light, and considering a side that we often ignore.

In some ways, this process was made easier for me because my father is dead. The dead are excellent listeners, and they never hurt us again by talking back. However, this exercise can be done in your journal no matter where your parents are, or if you never knew them at all. The same is true for other people who've shaped your self-worth. I'm confident that the time you spend on unearthing your issues around forgiveness will be well spent. The most important factor is simply your willingness to be true with yourself.

~

So my friend, take a chance. Come along on this journey. Consider a life of truth. Release your pain. Imagine that you have a choice. Don't be scared. I am here, and I am hurting too. I promise. I am way flawed, and I am still saved. Take hold of the only power that you will ever truly have, your own. Remember, you will not drown. You will breathe. I know it.

With much love and encouragement...
Your friend,
Nicole

# EPILOGUE

# The Stuff I Forgot to Say

"I guess I could be pretty pissed off about what happened to me... but it's hard to stay mad, when there's so much beauty in the world. Sometimes I feel like I'm seeing it all at once, and it's too much, my heart fills up like a balloon that's about to burst...

And then I remember to relax, and stop trying to hold onto it, and then it flows through me like rain, and I can't feel anything but gratitude for every single moment of my stupid little life.

You have no idea what I'm talking about, I'm sure.  But don't worry... you will someday."

Alan Ball
*American Beauty*

This book would not be complete without my favorite quote of all time: the last words spoken in the great film, *American Beauty*. I am saying this because the moment I heard it, it changed the way I saw everything in my life. I have been tortured by beauty, always. I have always felt trapped within the grips of my inability to feel it enough: The laughter and life in my children's eyes. A beloved friend's acknowledgment of my importance. An explosive fuchsia and orange sunset. The dance of the snow geese as they migrate back and forth across the sky. The raw sound of a stadium audience, as they sing along with an artist. The colors of the leaves as they change brilliantly, when suddenly summer turns to fall.

Beauty has always pained me, in these examples and infinite others. Yet, when Kevin Spacey spoke those words to me, I finally understood how to accept the pain. I had to see the truth of beauty: *Beauty cannot be held.*

If you try to hold onto it, you will hurt. I got this, and I felt it immediately. If I wanted to experience the joy of living with beauty, I would have to stop trying to hold it. I would have to breathe and release it, and allow it to "flow through me like rain." I was so young, but I got it.

This was, perhaps, my first real inkling of the meaning of truth as I see it today. It healed me without explanation. Appreciation is not a state of being, it is a byproduct of perspective.

I will, forever, be a student of truth and beauty.

# APPENDIX I

# Clients Speak

There is no group more inspired to shout from the rooftops than my client base. This is because they are all as desperate as I am to tell the world to WAKE UP.

Their lives, oftentimes having been set aside indefinitely as a result of chronic pain/conditions of all sorts, have been handed back to them with not only a renewed hope and energy, but with a vibrant new lens through which to view their futures. They are lawyers and manual laborers, bankers and clergy and holistic healers, producers and veterinary students. They are moms and dads, sons and daughters, caretakers and dependents. They fix mobile homes and take care of elderly people and mop the floors of universities. They herd children and manage hundreds of people at multinational corporations (same thing.) They are straight and gay and transgender and married and single and cheating and loyal. And, whomever they are, they are hurting far less than they used to.

~

*This is Olivia* (you guys have met):

I discovered Nicole's work at a time when I had basically given up hope on living any sort of normal life again. I was 23-years-old, and in so much pain and misery I couldn't get off the couch. Most days I didn't bother getting dressed. When my facial and head pain began, I was diagnosed with a slew of conditions like Trigeminal Neuralgia, Cluster Headaches, Migraine Disorders and New Daily Persistent Headache (NDPH). I was forced to defer veterinary school and move back into my mother's home, as I couldn't take care of myself. I left behind my boyfriend who had just moved across states to live with me in a new city and job. I spent every day of the next year in excruciating pain and agony, and feeling like I was a science experiment.

I traveled around the country to see various specialists at top institutions that were all trying to figure out what the hell was wrong with me. No luck. I was hospitalized for weeks at a time in several different states, with a variety of drugs pumped into my veins and a multitude of diagnostic tests performed, all of which never touched the pain. I scarfed down even more medications when I was at home all with the goal of trying to at least decrease the pain to a more tolerable level. Nope. Every week I was adding a new medication, but I wasn't seeing any changes. All this did was turn me into a total zombie, but I still had the same amount of pain. I made extreme diet changes, tried different holistic therapies, and resorted to essentially giving up. Most days were spent on the couch wishing I would just die because I'd rather be dead than live this way. Throughout all of this my hair was falling out in chunks from the stress and meds, and my body had become so emaciated.

My father found another specialist in South Africa, so with hope and promise I traveled to a foreign country for 2 months to be experimented on again. I had more MRIs, medications changed and added, surgeries on my face and skull, instruments put into my mouth, hospitalizations, and huge needles inserted deep into the various muscles of my head/face in attempts to find the source. I was terrified, sick and alone in Africa. Nothing was working and we had spent all of this money to save my life. I traveled back to the U.S. completely defeated, and still in so much pain.

When I found Dr. Sarno's work and Nicole Sachs' innovative and unique form of psychotherapy, my life began to change. Nicole threw all of herself into her work and my healing, and I felt from the beginning that she not only knew that I would be pain-free if I followed her teachings, but that I would get a new shot at my life. I journaled passionately and daily, following her program and purging myself of the anger and shame and self-loathing that has been festering inside me for a lifetime. I threw myself open to be gutted, and found that I could be loved for exactly who and what I am. I know it seems insane that these activities would cure me of chronic pain, but they did. Nothing else could touch my pain. Nicole's methods have absolutely healed it.

I have been able to go to vet school (going into 3rd year!), get engaged, enjoy the things I love again, and be successful in my life on my own terms. Yes, it is daily work for me, but I am so unbelievably grateful for this gift to view the world and myself in a way that my life before never gave me. I was trapped and suffering WELL BEFORE I got sick and found this journey; I just didn't know it. Today, thanks to Nicole and this wonderful work, not only am I am rid of all the meds, doctors, extreme treatments, fear and pain, but even better, I am free.

*This is Frankie*:

I read Nicole Sachs' words and felt instantly connected to her. I resonated with the passion and depth of her anguish to overcome pain and anxiety. She opened her soul and let me inside her world like no one else ever had. She was honest, intimate, bold and sassy. I wanted to know more about how this irreverent, feisty, funny and brilliant woman managed to find the courage to overcome her pain.

So I took the big plunge. I learned the art of personal excavation, getting into the mud of my stuff, uncovering parts of me that needed to be brought out into the sunlight. Nicole doesn't just listen; she digs right alongside of me as a steadfast partner in my explorations sharing her own stories and letting me know that I am not alone on this journey. I now have a trusty set of tools to assist me: journaling, meditating, visualizing, meaningful dialogue. With these I have learned how to stay strong, trust myself and know that all storms pass.

So what has all of this digging got me? I found sticky uncomfortable feelings and messy memories that were buried deep inside me. When I confronted those emotions bravely, I realized they had been causing me numerous health problems. The more I dug the more I released, and soon years of sciatic pain, swollen ankles, knee pain, muscle spasms, numbness and tingling in my back, legs and feet began to disappear. This personal work (with the guidance of Nicole's theories) was able to accomplish what surgery, epidural cortisone injections, physical therapy, acupuncture, massage and medications could not alleviate. I am still digging, but with a renewed sense of adventure and confidence that I have gained through my work with Nicole to whom I will be eternally grateful. So grab your shovel, lean in, and do the work; it just might be the magic you need to feel better than ever.

*This is Ingrid*:

As a child of sexual and physical abuse, I had never felt safe in my entire life. Not once. Not for a moment. With Nicole's book and her transformative theories of therapy, I finally felt the freedom that true safety brings. When you find that possibility, that space, you can finally heal. You can lay your weapon down and get on with the business of life, love, happiness and presence. Trust me, she will show you how - because even in book form you will see her love and humanity.

After 7 years in analysis with my former therapist in which she "listened and wrote down everything that I said," I entered into a disastrous second marriage, drank too much, treated my kid like shit and basically didn't have the life I wanted so desperately to have - and the one I thought I was fighting for so hard in therapy. I now know that this was because I never felt that I had a true advocate with a concrete plan to give me the bravery to change my life. I had chronic foot and leg pain, migraines and irritable bowel disease. I was living, but I was living small.

When I discovered Nicole's work and allowed it to shake the foundation of the "truths" I thought I had down pat, I was literally amazed at all the crap I was stuffing down. No wonder my body was so sick. I can only hope that people are ready to hear what Nicole has to say. She's saying something that every hurting human needs to hear, and do, in order to finally live again.

*This is Ricky*:

Although Dr. Sarno's books saved my life, Nicole Sachs' work helped me to understand why I needed to read his books in the first the place. I learned from her that there's something that goes even deeper in to the understanding of my pain, something that explains it ALL. That something is facing "the truth" about what we are truly feeling (not consciously thinking but feeling) no matter how awful that truth may be. The kind of truth that we repress deep in our unconscious mind. This kind of truth is hard to find in ourselves and even harder to face. Nicole shows us how to do both by bravely writing her own shocking example. By digging out her truth and exposing it, her unconscious mind couldn't use it to cause her physical pain anymore. This is fantastic and I've used her methods to help myself when I've needed more than Dr. Sarno's principles.

For many years I've searched for a "real" therapist. Someone who could actually answer my questions and explain things that are bothering me. Someone I could feel comfortable with and say anything to. But I never found anyone like that until I found Nicole. I've learned a lot about myself from her but what stands out most to me is how to understand what it is that I'm really feeling.

I was on disability for 7 years before I found Nicole's theories. My back pain, which I was so certain was "real" as a result of MRIs showing several bulging and slipped disks as well as arthritis at the base of my spine, completely resolved after 7 months of difficult soul-searching work. My life, the life I had relinquished, is back in my grasp. I am only 32 years old, and I had given up. Now I am back to work full-time and I've never felt more confident that I have a real future. I am alive.

~◡ノ

These people are you, and they are free. They are me, and they are living. There is no way out, other than through. I've helped these people through, and now they are able to thrive in their own lives. Might you be worth the effort?

# APPENDIX II

# Landing a Fab Therapist

I can be your therapist on these pages and in my energy and spirit, but we all know that I can't sit with each of you, personally. So, I agreed with some of my trusted advisors that it was a good idea to include a few pointers on therapist shopping, should that seem like the right path for you. Therapy is not very effective without a good fit between client and clinician. Since (although in our essence we are the same) we are all so different in our up-bringings, experiences, world-views, etc., there is no one type of therapist that would be right for everyone. Hence, here are a few things to keep in mind as you seek the person to help guide you.

1) Psychology Today (www.psychologytoday.com) is a great place to begin. Just click on *Find a Therapist* and it will allow you to enter your Zip Code to search in your area. Don't be creeped out by this, like it's online dating (not that there is anything wrong with that, either!) Nevertheless, people sometimes think that online connections with other people are not as genuine as other ways in which to connect. In the case of this site, I believe that the caliber of clinicians and the professionalism of the site are both very high. Many of my clients found me this way, when I first established my practice.

2) Whether you choose to go this route, or if you have another preferred method of searching, take a good look at the therapist's

philosophy, and how he or she describes it in detail. Psychology Today has a profile page for each practitioner, and most therapists are more than happy to have a brief phone call prior to starting treatment, in order to discuss the kind of work they do.

3) Don't be scared to ask any appropriate questions that come to mind. You are the authority on you, so if you need to know any specific details about the therapist's methods and practice in order to feel at ease, you should ask. Worst case scenario, the therapist will politely decline to answer. This will give you information in itself, depending on what you need in order to be comfortable.

4. If you have read this book and really believe that this is the path for you, or even if it simply made you curious enough to give it a go and hope for the best, ask prospective therapists if they have read it or if they would be willing to. Ask if they would feel comfortable guiding you toward your truths. My sincere hope is that many, many will. There is nothing to be scared of, for either of you.

The most important thing to hold onto is that you are important. Be true to yourself, and let your life unfold.

# Acknowledgements

T hank you,

Dr. Sarno, for your modest yet incomparable brilliance. Dr. John Garrick, for inspiring me to believe that I could be extraordinary. Dr. Mari Ann Graham, for giving me permission to think for myself. Dr. Anne Gearity, for teaching me to honor human development, and being so human herself when it came to my own child. Linda Jame, LCSW for being smart enough to trust, and always knowing exactly what I needed to hear.

Thank you,

Meri for listening to endless hours of my secrets when I trusted no one else. Meredith Sch., for being a true example of positive energy, despite life's circumstances. Jen, for having a fancy lunch bag, dispensing no-bullshit advice, and allowing me to be one of the few who truly see her. Mike, for liking me the best, and for coming to Seder despite family tragedy. Ronit, for being the most generous person I've ever met, in every way. Tracy, for your trust and truth, and your priceless input. Julianne, for making me laugh 'til I pee, and having the best stories, esp. the pantry experience. Cathy, for her unending kindness and loyal friendship. Sally, for loving my hair, and in turn encouraging me to love myself. Stacy, for loving your bulldogs and your nanny without apology.

Thank you,

Carolyn Francis, for offering unique friendship which has sustained for 20 years, a world apart. Ginny Peluso, for knowing shit you couldn't possibly know. The Peige & Scott Feldman and Linda & Mort Bender, and Ned R. Sachs for seeing beyond the ordinary.

Thank you to Dr. David B. Sachs, for exceeding all of my expectations, and becoming the friend and parent I'd always envisioned. Lock it up.

Thank you to Ellie Sugarman, for being the best, first (non)client a therapist could ask for. To Eric for letting me, and to Kiki and Cassie for inviting me to babysit.

Thank you to Allison DeLesia for being brave before I was, Greg Ackner for tolerating me, and Piper Ackner for always being the most excited person on the planet to see "Auntie Cole."

Thank you to the staff at Half Full in Lewes, DE (Emily, Isabel, Stacy) for welcoming me week after week during the writing of the first edition of this manuscript.

Thank you to Lizzie Pants Weber, for being the strongest woman I've ever met.

Thank you to every one of my clients, for your trust and your truth. You created this book.

Thank you Mommy, for a lifetime of truth, kindness and acceptance.

Thank you, thank you... my sweet little (big) perfect (imperfect) family. You fuel me, you lift me; you teach me. Isabella, Duncan, Oliver, Stella, Charlotte. You are kind and true and loving. What a gift. Special thanks to Isabella. One day you will realize the gravity of this book, as it pertains to your life. My love for you is infinite.

Tiffy. Your spirit and energy are so beautiful that they defy words. I can never find adequate ones. Thank you, my love, for gently and unknowingly giving me permission to be myself, and then loving that person without condition.

Michel Ferber (1946-1999) - You have no idea what you've done. Or, maybe you do. I have no need for assurance, however, as I know what I see. And I see you. Thank you, Daddy. I love you, and I forgive you.

## NOTES

1.  Prior to his retirement from NYU/Rusk earlier this year, Dr. Sarno provided his patients a monthly forum in which they could gather together and hear the stories of others who had overcome many painful chronic conditions through his practice and their guided personal work, and ask questions of the panel members.

2.  Dr. Sarno's contention that our brains "defend" us from painful subconscious thoughts is a key concept in his theories. The book that opened my eyes: John Sarno, *Healing Back Pain: The Mind-Body Connection*. Warner Books, 1991.

3.  Charles Darwin. *On the Origin of Species by Means of Natural Selection*. 1859.

4.  Rosie O'Donnell Show. Episode with Janette Barber, Rosie's producer at the time who overcame chronic pain which had her confined to a wheelchair, with the help of Dr. John Sarno's theories.

5.  Dr. John Sarno practiced at the The Rusk Institute of Rehabilitation Medicine at NYU (now called Rusk Rehab at NYU Langone Medical Center) when I saw him in May, 2005.

6.  Peter Block. *The Answer to How is Yes: Acting on What Matters*. Berrett-Koehler, 2001.

7.  The general concept of the three lists came from my personal meetings with Dr. John Sarno, and are highlighted in his book, *The Mindbody Prescription: Healing the Body, Healing the Pain*. Warner Books, 1998.

75596894R00119

Made in the USA
Columbia, SC
18 September 2019